WHAT PEOPLE ARE SAYING ABOUT

Tails from Beyond the Paw Print

"This is a heartwarming book. The author is one of the most caring pet lovers we have ever known. Over the years she has been in contact with us about her dear cats who were dying or had just passed on. The individual life stories on these pages are a testament to all who have lost a beloved pet. It will be hard for any reader to keep from weeping when being reminded of similar losses.

People who have lost beloved pets of any kind will recognize the heartfelt emotions that we all experience. These tales of beloved pets will help ease your own sense of loss. So many bereaved people are afraid of 'letting go'. They think it is letting go of the love and memories. But it really is the releasing of only the sharp edge of the pain, so we can go on with our lives. As this wonderful book shows, our beloved pets are a permanent part of us, and they stay forever in our hearts, enriching and blessing us.

We at the Association for Pet Loss and Bereavement recommend it for your permanent library."

— Wallace Sife, Ph.D., Author, The Loss of Pet; Founder APLB

"Between these covers are love stories. And, as in all true love stories, the tears will come – and the laughter catches you completely off-guard. Like in *The Velveteen Rabbit*, something happens inside us when we find the things that are real. There is 'real' here. This book is for anyone who has deeply loved an animal companion and mourned their loss. You will find kindred spirits here, friends who have walked where you are walking, and who will help you find a pathway to heal."

— Beverly M. Beltramo, D.Min, BCC, Director, Spiritual Care, Mission Integration, Ascension Hospital System, Michigan Market

"Every story in this book shows the powerful love that the 22 contributors felt for their animal companions. From the first story to the last, I couldn't help feeling a roller-coaster of emotions. We have all been there and this book is a strong reminder of the unconditional love that humans receive from their companions. As the CEO of the Michigan Humane Society, I have suffered loss, and each loss has taught me something that helps make an impact on another animal's life. As difficult as it is to say goodbye, the memories and the lessons learned from each animal will remain with me forever. These memories are why I do what do.

This is an incredible book that every pet owner and animal advocate should read. The stories told are raw and full of emotion. Thank you to Dr. Micky Golden Moore for founding Beyond the Paw Print and for turning her dream into a reality - sharing this selection of stories by past and present group members into a book that every animal lover can relate to."

— Matthew Pepper, President and CEO, Michigan Humane Society

"Bravely confronting her own unreconciled losses, both human and animal companion, Micky Golden Moore was determined to uncover the roadblocks that kept her knee-deep in pain – both physical and emotional. Her profound desire to help others led her from academia to chaplaincy, from the classroom to the bedside, and ultimately to the creation of Beyond the Paw Print. After experiencing the loss of her own beloved animal companions, Micky discovered a general lack of support for this form of grief by the greater community. She sought refuge in the creation of a pet loss support group to reach those who might otherwise grieve in isolation. This book is a tribute to those who have ever loved and lost a beloved animal companion. Past and present Beyond the Paw Print attendees courageously share their journey from hello to goodbye, relaying the lessons learned along the way. Discover how this group has created a safe haven to share grief and heal wounded hearts."

— Howard Schubiner, MD, Internal Medicine,
Program on Mind Body Medicine, Ascension Providence Hospital

"As a veterinarian for more than 40 years, I've seen an amazing change in how we live with our pets. From the barn or backyard to the couch, they now frequently join us in our beds. That change of course is emblematic of where our pets fit in our lives. For many, these creatures are a major pillar for mental and emotional well-being.

So, it's no surprise that pet loss can be a devastating event, which is why this book is so important. Each story takes us on a journey from first hello through goodbye. Through her work with hundreds of bereaved pet owners, Dr. Golden Moore lovingly draws back the curtain to reveal the phenomenal bond between humans and their companions, how we can make meaning of our losses, and discover that we can transform our grief. I know of no other person more gifted and qualified to help us understand that relationship."

— David J. Whitten DVM. Hilldale Veterinary Hospital, Southfield, MI

"I have known Micky for over ten years since her inception of this noble and heartfelt calling to provide counseling and a place to share our suffering and express our joy and love for our furry friends. The stories are touching, heartfelt, and full of optimism, as all these people, through their grief, rise resilient with strength and joy to provide hope for others missing their special friends.

The Beyond the Paw Print Support Group is an invaluable gift for people who were isolated and paralyzed by the grief of losing their animal family members and had no one to turn to or understand what they were experiencing. It emphasizes human kinship in supporting one another through the loss of our furry friends. A sincere thank you to Dr. Golden Moore for her tireless commitment in bringing this book to life. What joy and peace this book will bring to so many people! I wholeheartedly recommend it to anyone experiencing the loss of these extraordinary family members."

—Anna Luisa Di Lorenzo MD FACS, Professor, Oakland University William Beaumont School of Medicine

"No one can truly understand the gut-wrenching pain experienced by a pet owner who has to say goodbye to their loving companion. The unconditional love and acceptance we get from our pets can transcend that of the closest human relationships. Our 'four legged children' fill our days with love, laughter, affection, and the purest loyalty and devotion that only an animal can provide. They let us know in countless ways that they will be there for us no matter what the circumstances. So when they are no longer there, the ensuing void can permeate our entire lives.

The pain of coming home to an empty house without their joyful presence to greet us can feel unbearable. Only another pet lover who has experienced such a devastating loss can possibly comprehend the depth of our pain. Dr. Micky Golden Moore's new book is truly a gift for anyone who has ever known the love of an animal and had to say goodbye much too soon."

— Sue Levine, Production Coordinator, RWL/The WW Group

"Losing a pet is nothing short of heartbreaking. For many of us, pets are beloved members of our family. When we have to say goodbye, they take a piece of our hearts with them that we really never get back. There is a void left behind that is unable to be filled and the grief sometimes feels too heavy a burden to bear.

Finding comfort in others who share the same love and bond and knowing that there are kindred spirits who truly understand our pain, can bring us the peace and support we need during such a difficult time.

Tails from Beyond the Paw Print will make you smile, laugh, and cry all at once but even more importantly, it will help you realize you are not alone. This book is an excellent reminder to us all how important it is to talk about our grief, remember our beloved pets, and honor their memories in whatever way we can."

— Corey Gut, DVM, Veterinarian;
Author, *Being Brave for Bailey* and *Staying Strong for Smokey*

"For those of us who have been blessed to know the love of an animal, it is truly the purest form of love. The bonds we build with our pets over their lifetimes are incredibly meaningful. They teach us so many wonderful lessons in life. They help us, they read us, they comfort us, and they support us. Our animals are by our sides through all of life's joys and sorrows.

Tails from Beyond the Paw Print will make you feel all the emotions we experience with a pet – pure joy, love, playfulness, support, and eventually incredible loss. Micky has truly shared wonderful, heartfelt stories that will fill you with emotion and love. This healing book will help you work through the grief and find some peace after losing a beloved animal family member. Pet loss is a devastating experience and I am grateful that Micky has written this book to help."

— Karlene Belyea, MBA, Chief Culture Officer, Mission Veterinary Partners, Former CEO, Michigan VMA

"Owning and working in a pet store for nearly three decades, I have had the privilege of meeting and serving tens of thousands of customers through the wonders, trials, and tribulations of pet ownership. Our customers and their companions have made an imprint on my life and that of my staff. Unfortunately, when a customer's companion dies, we too, feel a sense of loss when we never see that customer or companion again.

I have personally struggled with my own pet loss grief, and it's extremely tough. For many of us, our pets are so much more than just pets. They are members of our family, and there is nothing more painful than losing a family member. Beyond the Paw Print Pet Loss Support group and its founder, Dr. Micky Golden Moore provide the kindness and understanding that every grieving pet owner needs. Tails from Beyond the Paw Print is a necessity for every pet owner. The stories in this book provide reassurance, comfort, and hope as we navigate our way through pain, loss, and grief."

Mike Palmer, Owner, Premier Pet Supply

Although an organization, book, or website is noted in this work, the listing does not mean the publisher endorses the information that the organization or Website may provide or the recommendations it makes. Please note: Websites listed in this work may have changed between when this work was written and when it is read.

This publication is designed to provide information related to the subject matter covered. If expert assistance or counseling is needed, the services of a competent professional should be sought.

Printer: Sheridan Books
Printed in the United States of America
Design and Art Direction: Eric Keller Design
Illustrations: Hannah Tegan Johnson
Editor in Chief: Cindi Cook
Editorial Manager: Micky Golden Moore
Production Design: Arlene Cohn
Project coordinator: Micky Golden Moore
Proofreaders: Bud Moore, Patty Merlo, Kelly Rhoades, Beverly Beltrano, Howard Schubiner
Set in: Whitman Roman, Parkinson Roman, and Seria Pro

Moore, Micky Golden
Tails from Beyond the Paw Print: Twenty-Two Stories of Love, Loss, and Lessons Learned from our Adored Animal Companions

ISBN number: 978-0-9600281-0-8

TAILS FROM BEYOND THE PAW PRINT

Twenty-two stories of love, loss, and lessons learned from our adored animal companions

MICKY GOLDEN MOORE, Ph.D., M.S.H.P.

ILLUSTRATIONS BY HANNAH TEGAN JOHNSON

PUBLISHED BY BEYOND THE PAW PRINT, L.L.C.

To Bud, the love of my life.
With you, everything is possible.

This book is dedicated to:

Anyone who has ever loved and lost a member of the animal kingdom.

The 21 participants who bravely permitted me to share their stories of love, loss and lessons learned. Without them, this book would not exist.

Those, who in search of comfort, community, and validation in their grief, shared their stories at a Beyond the Paw Print Meeting or with our online group.

In loving memory of my parents, Louis and Sylvia Golden. They believed in my dreams and encouraged me to write about my adventures with Pablo, Nellie, and Isabella.

In loving memory of my sweet Pablo, the inspiration for Beyond the Paw Print Pet Loss Support Group and this book.

P = Purrrfectly Pleasing
A = Adorable and Accepting
B = Best Buddy
L = Lessons About Love
O = One and Only

Contents

"Until one has loved an animal,
a part of one's soul remains unawakened."

—Anatole France

PATCHY

Foreword

By Dr. Kelly Rhoades

If you have never opened your heart to experience the depth of love in the human-animal bond, then perhaps you shouldn't open this book at all. We who love our pets know that at our core, there need be no explanation for this abiding emotion, this unconditional acceptance in the purest form of delightful companionship. Those of us who adore our animals are often referred to as mere enthusiasts by non-pet owners, and sometimes harshly judged because we love these four-legged creatures so deeply. Can you imagine being judged for that? I don't understand it. It's a love that goes far beyond enthusiasm.

Loving deeply includes the risk of loss, and in the case of a pet, we know from the very first meeting that we will only have them for a little while. Yet still, we throw ourselves back in, over and over, to take in a new furry friend because it is the purest kind of love there is. The difficulty comes in that as much as we love, so too do we grieve. Pets are family members, providing us with constant comfort, stability, and a refuge from everyday stressors. The unexpected and devastating sorrow from the death of a beloved animal companion may be surprising for some, and perhaps even a reason to question one's sanity.

Statements can often come from those around us like, "It's "just a dog" or "just a cat" … "What's happening to you?" or "Why can't you just get a new pet?" These responses deepen the divide between us and well-intended others.

Let's be very clear, I am not working toward cementing the division that seems to persist in our society, as in the pet lover vs. non-pet lover; indeed, quite to the contrary. I'm promoting connection and a better understanding between the two sides, because in this modern world, we have plenty of divisiveness and disconnection. What I am proposing are the elements necessary for finding our way through the very real sadness that follows after a beloved pet dies, and to acknowledge why Beyond the Paw Print Pet Loss Support Group was formed in the first place: to find a safe forum to express the depth of feelings in losing one's pet, and to find connection with other grieving people in various phases of their bereavement. This group offers hope that healing communities exist and can help us with the sometimes scary and overwhelming amount of grief that we experience when a pet dies. It is very real.

This book is about telling our stories. Dr. Golden Moore is the founder and has been the facilitator for over ten years now of this profound grief support group. "Micky," as we all eventually come to call her, combines her skill sets of interpersonal communication and grief counseling to provide a place where we all gather to tell our stories and receive unconditional love, acceptance, kindness, and connection in the sanctuary of a healing community. She has created the perfect formula for effective grief support!

Micky came to my classroom – a graduate level bereavement theory course – in the winter of 2008, asking (emphatically, of course) if her required class project could "please, please, please" be about "pet loss support." Micky had entered the graduate program in Hospice and Palliative studies in the autumn of 2007, still reeling over the death of her parents. The reason for her desire to research the subject of pet loss arose from personal experience. The health of her three senior cats, Pablo, Isabella, and Nellie, had declined, and Micky did her best to prepare for the journey to goodbye and wanted to immerse herself in the subject. She was bursting at the seams with grief over the death of her parents and the anticipatory grief of her three companions, true, but she was also bursting with energy and vitality for life!

Micky explained to me at her interview for graduate program entry that her strengths reside deep within her soul and are based on her father's philosophy that had in turn formed their family's legacy. It's one that believes that we are our brother's keeper and that life is a precious gift. Micky's greatest strength, she explained, was her desire to help others, something she fully attributes to her parents. They instilled in her an awareness and sensitivity to the human spirit that has informed her life tremendously. Micky drew readily from this deep desire to help others through the pain of her own grief, and very openly shared her feelings for all to see by completing this very personal project in my classroom. It did not end there. This classroom assignment evolved because of her tenacity and caring heart, and came to fruition in Beyond the Paw Print.

Validation, safety, witnessing, sanctuary, comfort, healing, and ultimately celebration are essential factors needed for life to begin again with the renewed perspective of possibilities. As we fully explore the meaning of our loss, we do eventually move out of the depths of despair with renewed perspective and an appreciation for what remains. This renewal of spirit brings joy as we continue sharing the memories and stories of our beloved companion animal. We then look to the possibilities that will happen when we transform our grief. This processing brings the kind of wholeness that can only come from the choice to feel deeply the emotions of loss while climbing out of the abyss to reach joy, find peace, and to love again, perhaps more deeply than before. Climbing out however, cannot be done alone. We need a healing community, and a place to connect with others who understand without judgment, who welcome the tears that come through our stories. Those memories then become the relationship that we have forever with our pet. This heart felt connection does not die.

Life is filled with uncertainties. Social science researcher Dr. Brené Brown teaches us that our "beauty lies in our vulnerability." I believe Micky continues to remind all of us to dig deep and keep our hearts open, no matter how hard our tale might be to tell. The stories she handed me in a binder, written by 21 past and present attendees of BTPP, were all in draft form, filled with evidence of this hardship. Yes, I agreed to the task at hand, that is, to write the foreword for this book. We established a due date but what I failed to grasp in those initial meetings (and with all of my expertise as a grief counselor, I might add), is that I was still very raw in my feelings over the death of my own beloved twelve-year-old English Setter, Patchy. I started reading the stories and cried through each one. Not able to continue at the pace I had naively envisioned, I had to put the drafts down, and take time out to breathe, to process.

An important part of managing our grief usually brings us to the question about timing for a new pet. Is there a "right time" to acquire another one? I believe the answer to that question has to be aligned with your needs, comfort and lifestyle. It is absolutely an individual decision that is as unique as your grief, and a personal journey that's different for everyone. Listen to your heart. I did get a puppy just five months after our Patchy died. Our nine-week old English Setter, Lucas, (the name literally means "bringer of light") brought renewal and comfort to my broken heart. He kissed away my tears and brought such joy through his puppy antics. Lucas immediately assumed both comedic and soothing roles in my life, while teaching me, daily, to keep my heart open. It's important to note, he was not Patchy. We do not replace our pets, as is a common assumption. They all have unique personalities. I believe they choose us. Lucas, now two years old, is indeed the light of our lives, offering 75 pounds of pure lap dog love!

My summary for all of you who courageously shared experiences of your own loss in this book, or for those who are picking up this book for the first time: Do not let the pain of reading these stories scare you away. What follows are messages written from places of deep grief. Talk about vulnerability! They are also beautiful testimonials of pure love. I am not going to sugar-coat this: These stories are not easy to read. It's not the sharing that brings the tears, it is, simply, the loss of our beloved pet. We're seeking comfort and understanding in our grief. I promise you will feel better after reading this wonderful book. That is the nature of grief: The only way through is through. We must go through it to heal. So, pace yourself, take deep breaths, and grab some tissues, but keep reading. We cry because we recognize our own story of loss, but perhaps even more profoundly, we feel the depth of this kind of pure love in the loss of our beloved animal companion. We heal by telling each other our heartfelt stories. Micky has given us this forum.

I miss my sweet Patchy every day, still, after two years. I wonder sometimes, does anyone know how deeply I loved him? Does anyone really know how amazing this dog was? Does anyone care? I am comforted as I recall the silliness, the joy, the laughter, the love, and of course, the 75 pounds of pure lap dog pleasure he brought to me, sprawled out in my corner chair each night. He would quietly and peacefully lay his head on my shoulder, and very simply love me. How do you ever say good-bye to that?

Well… we somehow do. We must. We have to go on to honor their lives. We learn to love again, continue to open our hearts, and to remember our beautiful companions with less pain over time. This legacy of memory keeps us connected to the gifts that they gave us while alive. I believe they become our guardian angels in spirit, forever watching over us. Our human-animal connections become the sweet love stories of devotion that cannot possibly be fully understood by others. As pet lovers, and yes, pet enthusiasts – may we invite all of you who are not, to curb the judgment and open your hearts to what I described earlier as an unconditional acceptance and love in the purest form of delightful companionship, because who wouldn't want to experience that?

With gratitude for the connection created within healing communities, and for all of our animal companions who watch over us.

Dr. Kelly Rhoades, Retired Chair and Professor,
Hospice and Palliative Studies Department,
Madonna University
Livonia, Michigan
Author, *Quilly's Sideways Grief*

"What is Real?" asked the Rabbit one day. "Does it mean things that buzz inside you and a stick-out handle?"

"Real isn't how you are made," said the Skin Horse. "It's a thing that happens to you.

When a child loves you a long, long time, not just to play with, but REALLY loves you, then you become Real."

"Does it hurt?" asked the rabbit. "Sometimes," said the Skin Horse, for he was always truthful.

"When you are Real you don't mind being hurt."

"Does it happen all at once, like being wound up," he asked, "Or bit by bit?"

"It doesn't happen all at once," said the Skin Horse. You become…"

— Margery Williams,
The Velveteen Rabbit

NELLIE
Kensington
PABLO
Isabella

Introduction

by Micky Golden Moore, Ph.D., M.S.H.P.

Months of planning hadn't eased the self-doubt that threatened to overwhelm me as I entered the classroom I had rented at a local church for the first Beyond the Paw Print Pet Loss Support Group meeting on March 9, 2009. Fueled with nervous energy, I arrived two hours early with a car full of grief support resources and hoped there would be sufficient time to set up all these "must have" items. After several trips between my car and the classroom, the next task was to create an atmosphere where attendees would feel that their pet loss grief was both recognized and validated. After arranging the chairs in a semicircle, I placed the dozens of books, pamphlets, and handouts on the subject of pet loss, grief, and healing on the tables that were set up against the wall. Among the handouts were the BTPP meeting guidelines and mission statement, hot off the press, and ready to be distributed to each attendee. Most important, I placed several boxes of tissues within easy reach of the seats. Outside the classroom, I set up a check in table with a sign-in sheet, name tags, and markers. I re-entered the classroom and adjusted the display areas a second time. Then I stopped, took a look around, and froze. I was suddenly overcome with anxiety and insecurity. In an effort to calm myself, I took deep breaths and tried to think positively. When that failed, I closed my eyes, reached deep within, and felt compelled to pray.

I prayed with gratitude for all the individuals whose encouragement and support gave me the courage to create this support group. I prayed with gratitude for Pablo, Nellie, and Isabella, the three felines whom I loved with a devotion I never knew possible, and in whose memory this group was created. I prayed that BTPP would serve those individuals seeking acknowledgment and support for the loss of their beloved animal companions. I prayed that attendees would join me in creating a compassionate and caring community. And I prayed that attendees would find healing.

Then I prayed that the few individuals who had reserved a seat would actually show up for this, the very first meeting.

With an hour to spare, I alternated between pacing the room, rearranging the resource materials, and staring out the window which overlooked the parking lot. A few minutes later, my husband arrived. In a show of support, a few of our friends walked through the door, and minutes later, much to my surprise, our veterinarian also came in. Their presence filled my heart with gratitude. The clock ticked, and while the small group chitchatted, I reviewed my introductory remarks, just in case someone showed up for the meeting. Then it happened: one at a time, people began to arrive!

While they reviewed the handouts and pet loss materials, I hoped the attendees felt reassured that they had come to the right place. As the clock approached the start time, I invited the attendees to take their seats, and in a further show of support, my husband found a seat within the semi-circle. Our personal posse of caring friends took their leave, and… *I was NOT ready to begin!*

I stood before the group and my heart raced, my throat closed up, and tears filled my eyes. The moment I had anticipated and planned for had finally arrived, yet I felt frozen, immobile. I pushed myself through the anxiety, fear, and panic, recalling the reasons that I had created BTPP – to listen, support, and validate those grieving the death of their animal companions and to create a space where attendees would feel safe sharing their stories and their tears. I sought to provide a refuge for those who had been grieving in isolation; a port in the storm where attendees might find kinship, kindness, and community. Ultimately, my objective was for attendees to rediscover hope and begin the healing process. These reminders put the focus where it belonged – on the individuals in those seats. *And so, I found the courage to speak.*

With those teary eyes and a tentative voice, I welcomed the attendees to the very first meeting of the Beyond the Paw Print Pet Loss Support Group. After I reviewed the meeting guidelines, I volunteered to be the first member of our group to share a story, specifically, Pablo's story. In that very moment, I realized if these individuals were brave enough to attend the meeting with the intention of sharing their stories, I should be willing to share mine too. I should allow my tears to fall in this unique forum of strangers, gathered together because of our shared love for and grief over the death of a beloved animal companion. Shouldn't I serve as an example that yes, healing is indeed possible? So, I opened the meeting with an abbreviated version of Pablo's story (Story 22), and described how his love, constant presence, and yes, his death, transformed me and gave me the courage to create this group. When I finished, I invited group members to share their story.

As the meeting progressed, I witnessed a change in the room. A sense of unspoken trust enabled each attendee to share their stories and express their grief. I was struck by their openness, their willingness to be vulnerable, and the raw emotion that was evident as they spoke. After the meeting, I was amazed when attendees stayed behind to express their gratitude for the establishment of this group. Their reaction served as an inspiration, and I was committed to learn how to best spread the word so that others would know that support was available.

As I reflect back on the events that led to that first meeting, my journey wasn't straightforward or simple, yet each twist and turn led to my role in the field of pet loss grief support.

Nothing in my life prepared me for grief. In fact, I studiously avoided feelings of grief, loss, and mourning. As a young adult and college student, my focus had been the study of the human condition and human communication. I was fascinated by the research in these subjects, had a strong desire to improve my own fledgling skills, and found a home in the world of academia. Unable or unwilling to explore my lifelong difficulties with goodbyes and farewells, I focused on my academic career as a way to protect myself from life's tough stuff. That strategy didn't work so well on the day I learned that my dad was seriously ill.

My introduction to the world of hospitals, surgery, and complicated outcomes occurred in 1991, when my dad was diagnosed with kidney and colon cancer. His kidney was removed, and the surgery was considered a success. The colon cancer surgery, not so much.

We listened closely as the surgeon informed Dad that he would need to see an oncologist. This was the first time I had heard that term and was too embarrassed to ask the surgeon to provide a definition. I didn't broach the subject with my dad as I didn't want to upset him. "What's an oncologist?" I asked one of the nurses, later in the day, outside the room. The nurse responded, "it's a doctor who specializes in the treatment of cancer." My throat closed up and and I felt overwhelmed with fear.

My dad had always been the strongest person I knew. To me he was invincible. No matter the challenges, he made it through. Now he needed support. I had no idea what to do or how to help. Here I was, a communication major, without any idea how to express myself. I was unaware of what Dad needed most – a nonjudgmental, listening presence. I was light years away from these insights when I joined Dad, along with my siblings, on his extensive journey of treatments, remission, new diagnoses, further treatments, palliative care, and then finally, hospice care.

During my dad's initial illness and treatment, I adopted my feline companion, Pablo, and several months later, Isabella, and Nellie. Their presence would bring great comfort and lift my spirits. I had fallen off an emotional cliff and found a safety net in the love and affection of my feline family. With them, I could openly shed tears into their furry necks and receive comfort from their close proximity, cuddled in my arms, close to my heart. I don't know what I would have done without them.

As Dad's early treatments led to lengthy periods of remission, I completed my education, began work as an adjunct university instructor, and met my future husband. For the next several years, Dad continued on with great optimism, in the firm belief that his doctors would be able to resolve any ongoing setbacks to his health. Dad's optimism was contagious; it allowed me to embrace the future without fear, until his health began to decline.

My first encounter with a hospice chaplain occurred in 2002, when my dad's battle with cancer changed from curative to comfort care. Those final months were very difficult for him, and in mid-November 2002, Dad agreed to accept the services of a local hospice, where he received care at home. Although this was a very challenging time period, Dad found comfort from the hospice chaplains and spiritual care volunteers who regularly visited him. Moreover, their judgement-free presence and vast experience with end-of-life patients and their families, provided the reassurance we needed as we sought, individually and together, to navigate our way through this uncharted territory.

These experiences left an imprint on my heart, and I vowed that if I could make it through the loss of my dad, I would investigate the requirements of becoming a chaplain. I wanted to provide that same loving care for others, that had been provided for my dad. This dream was put on hold, as I wasn't prepared for the crippling effects of my grief when Dad died in 2003. Despite the love and care of my family – both human and feline, I struggled to find my footing. As with my previous struggles, my sweet Pablo, along with Isabella and Nellie were a continued source of comfort.

Then, on February 15, 2006, my beloved mom died, suddenly and unexpectedly. For more than one year after her death, I was inconsolable, stuck in the abyss of my grief. I couldn't move through my grief, let alone move forward. Once again, Pablo, Isabella, and Nellie, an ever-constant presence, became my bedrock of support – my comforters and confidantes.

Those close to me were concerned about my wellbeing. Nothing seemed to help. Then, I received a lifeline from Jennifer Cote, Chairwoman (now retired) of the Department of Paralegal Studies at Madonna University. Jennifer had provided legal services for my Mom and remained in touch after her death. Jennifer encouraged me to reach out to her colleague, Dr. Kelly Rhoades, Chairwoman of the Department of Hospice and Palliative Studies at the university. This connection changed my life. Entrance to this unique graduate program, with a concentration in Bereavement Studies, provided the hope, direction, and gateway to healing I so desperately sought. My Mom always said that when God closes a door, he opens a window. I believed that Mom's adage was true for me — a window had indeed been opened.

Dr. Rhoades was an excellent lecturer and I found the coursework fascinating. Though I silently wept through some of the more poignant lectures, I felt like I had found a home in this program. Initially, I sought to understand my own grief. As I found my footing, I rediscovered my passion to help others, although I was uncertain of the specific path I might follow.

In the midst of this program, the health of my now senior feline companions began to decline. As described in Pablo's story (Story 22), they were in treatment for a variety of senior cat maladies, but despite all efforts, they received their angel wings within months of each other.

After their deaths, I found myself, yet again, in the abyss of new grief. This time however, my grief was complicated. I was struck by the way this grief was often minimized or invalidated by others. I learned that pet loss grief is a form of disenfranchised grief; a loss not recognized or sanctioned as legitimate by the general public.

With each heart wrenching goodbye, the veterinary staff presented us with each of our cat's paw prints set in clay. As you can see in the photograph on the opening page of this introduction, the upper right portion of Nellie's heart-shaped paw print is broken. I chose to leave it unrepaired, as it aptly reflected the break in my heart at the time of her death. These clay paw prints remain treasured mementos, long after the floral arrangements dried out and the condolence cards from our veterinarians were filed away for safekeeping. In the initial aftermath of Nellie's, Pablo's, and Isabella's deaths, I often found myself handling their clay paw prints, a sort of linking object, that helped me feel connected to them in the absence of their presence.

Fortunately, I was in the right place to express my grief, and with the encouragement and support of Dr. Rhoades, I researched pet loss grief within her graduate seminar. I was struck by the depth and breadth of research that had been conducted in this field, and the idea for a pet loss support group was formed through this seminar. With each consecutive course, I gained the much-needed confidence to adapt the ideas described in my research papers and transform them into reality.

Three questions dominated my thoughts: Were there others grieving the deaths of animal companions in silence and isolation? Did they have a desire to share their stories? Would they be interested in attending a pet loss support group?

From my personal experience and informal polling of others, I felt encouraged that I was on the right track. With a passion I didn't know I possessed; I followed my heart toward the pursuit of my dream.

The next step; choosing a name for my group. This turned out to be easier than I anticipated. It came to me one morning after waking from a dream. I was thinking about the moment when other bereaved pet parents receive their clay paw print. Where might they turn if they desired additional support, beyond the paw print? When I said the name out loud – "Beyond the Paw Print" — it sounded just right, and the mission of my group became clear. *Beyond the Paw Print: Transforming the Pet Loss Experience*, was born.

I had no idea what to expect after that very first BTPP Support Group meeting. I didn't even know if there would be sufficient inquiries to hold a meeting the following month. But gradually, news began to spread, and the group has continued to grow and thrive. And yes, nearly eleven years later, I still feel tears in my eyes at the start of each meeting. I am grateful for these tears, as they remind me of where and how it all began.

My role as facilitator of the BTPP meetings has brought many unexpected gifts. Every meeting brings the opportunity to learn from the experiences of the attendees and has led me to become a better facilitator and a more compassionate listener. The meetings are the highlight of my month and I treasure the kinship and kindness that unite us in our search for healing. I am happy to welcome newcomers and returning attendees to the meetings, and even happier for the comfort and consolation they appear to find through the group.

The idea for a book began many years ago, when a story I wrote about Pablo was published in the Association for Pet Loss and Bereavement's online newsletter. Through the years, I often re-read Pablo's story and thought about the hundreds of stories that had been shared within the confines of the BTPP group meetings. I imagined that individuals outside our circle would benefit from these stories of love, loss, and lessons learned.

Equally important, I imagined that an expansion of these stories to the greater community could assist in changing the culture around pet loss.

With encouragement from those closest to me, I sent an email to past and present attendees with the subject heading, "BTPP is publishing a book and would love to include your story." I explained my idea and asked recipients if they had an interest in joining me. I was overwhelmed by the responses. Undeterred by the structure of my nine-step outline and other constraints that I described in excruciating detail, the drafts started arriving and I felt hopeful about the potential of this project. The following eighteen months were consumed with re-writes and edits of the 21 stories. Each of the contributors remained enthusiastic throughout the entire process, motivated by their desire to share the stories of their beloved companions. There were times, when overwhelmed by the self-publishing process and my own lack of experience, I floundered and feared that completion of *Tails from the Beyond the Paw Print* appeared an impossible and unattainable goal. But, little by little, step by step, we did it! The book is complete and has found its way to you and your tender hearts.

Each story follows a chronology beginning with the first hello through the final goodbye. But the stories don't end there. You will be led through each person's unique journey through grief, with a stop along the way at BTPP. This is not a "how to" or "should do" type of book. These stories, as the book title suggests, are stories of personal love, loss, and lessons learned. These stories, so bravely shared at the meetings, now belong to the greater community.

I invite you into the lives of these wonderful animals, along with the love and longing expressed in these stories by their human guardians. The illustrations that accompany each story, so caringly created by Hannah T. Johnson, capture each animal's essence, and may in turn, further capture your heart.

I consider each of these 21 contributors a dear friend and partner on the journey toward healing. Joining them on their unique journey has been life-changing for me. I hold them, their stories, and their lessons learned, lovingly in my heart.

"I carry your heart with me (I carry it in my heart)"

— e.e. cummings

ST. CLAIR

STORY ONE

An Unlimited Capacity for Love

By Steve

AT OUR FIRST MEETING, SHE PEED ON MY SHOE. At our second meeting, she bit my finger. At our third meeting, I knew she was meant for me.

I met St. Clair at a pet store when she was four months old. My partner and I had already owned a rescued Airedale but when I saw this sweet dog cooped up in that small crate, I knew I couldn't live with myself if I didn't get her out of there. Because I was acquainted with a local Airedale rescue, I sought their advice before buying her. What I learned didn't please me: St. Clair may have come from a puppy mill. The rescue offered their assistance if I decided to foster right away. During the process, I visited with St. Clair at the store each week. It took three weeks to finally bring her home — between working with the rescue, communicating with the store, and juggling my schedule.

St. Clair's name came about from my love of the lake and the many summers I spent boating, swimming, and simply enjoying the views and fresh air. I couldn't wait to introduce my new puppy to all of it. She wasn't the typical, over-the-top rambunctious Airedale; she was more sedate, really the perfect dog in so many ways. Potty training was accomplished in only a couple weeks, and at nine months old, St. Clair graduated from her crate, with free run of the house.

St. Clair was a wonderful companion and we attended many rescue functions around metro Detroit. We walked with rescue groups in parades and attended Airedale fundraisers. We were also regulars at grandma and grandpa's house where she was endlessly spoiled with treats and toys. Doggie Day Care centers were increasing in popularity around the time St. Clair was two years old. Of course, I wanted my sweet little angel to be one of the first clients to experience all the perks. For the next ten years, St. Clair enjoyed being a weekly client. She loved it and would give me "the eye" and follow me through the house every morning until I said, "Let's go to doggie daycare!" She would jump like a kangaroo all the way out to the car. Needless to say, the evenings afterward were very quiet as she was tuckered out from playing all day.

Fast-forward to the fall of 2016 and an unfortunate turn of events: St. Clair was diagnosed with Stage II kidney disease. I was determined to do something — anything — to help her. I began to research all I could in order to prevent the disease from advancing. Despite various protocols and treatments led by our vet and other specialists, I soon recognized that St. Clair was on borrowed time. When saying goodnight, which I did every night by holding her close, I told St. Clair that if she was ready to leave, I understood and that she could go in her sleep. She apparently wanted to stay.

About six months later, something in St. Clair's eyes told me that she was no longer feeling well. People said she would "let me know" when it was time to say goodbye, and I recognized that the time was approaching. She had beds on every floor of the house but loved the basement and was still able to manage the stairs. Her appetite had diminished as a result of the kidney disease and other ailments. I kept changing her food to stimulate her appetite. Her desire to go on her daily walks remained strong, even though she could only go around the block.

Early one Saturday morning, I heard St. Clair barking and I immediately went downstairs to see how she was doing. I became upset when I saw that she had a few accidents in the basement. I raised my voice and scolded her. We then went outside and suddenly she laid down and started trembling. I was worried but I had two appointments that I needed to keep, and felt reassured that my partner would keep a close eye on her. Despite checking on St. Clair throughout the day, it was apparent that by the late afternoon, we had to go to the emergency room.

St. Clair had made it back downstairs, but by this time, she was unable to walk. We made a hammock out of a comforter to get her into the car. I can still picture her looking right at me as if to say, "Thank you Dad, I'm so sick." At the hospital, they told me her kidney values were off the charts. After they stabilized her, I apologized for the way I had treated her that morning. I have never cried so hard in my life.

They needed an ultrasound, but the tech had left for the day and wouldn't be back until Monday. Every four hours I called to get an update. I visited St. Clair the next morning as soon as I could. She was able to walk into the room on her own; I was overjoyed. I apologized again for my actions the previous morning. We spent some time just looking at and being with each other. When I called a little while later, the vet told me that St. Clair had been quite upset after I left, as she wanted to go with me. I didn't go back to see her that evening to allow her to rest, but continued to phone the vet hospital to check on her condition.

On Monday morning, I called for an update and learned that she was going in for an ultrasound. At 2:00 p.m., the doctor called and explained that they had found some spots on her spleen and kidney, and an abscess on her liver appeared to have burst. There were also signs that appeared to be lymphoma on other parts of her body. Then he uttered the dreaded words — humane euthanasia. I was already out the door from work while still on the phone with him, asking about other options. My partner met me at the hospital and after another consultation, we decided that euthanizing her would, at that point, be best. I've had bad days in my life, but this was the worst. I signed the papers and held her head in my arms, my face by hers, whispering in her ear that I loved her until the doctor said she had died.

We made arrangements with a local crematory to have a private cremation the next day. At the crematory, they took us into a room where St. Clair was in a white box. Although this was incredibly difficult, it was simultaneously comforting to see her one last time to say goodbye.

I placed a red rose under her paws that rested on her face. The attendants came in and loaded St. Clair's coffin into the crematory and asked if I wanted to push the button to start the process. I did. The cremation process took about two and a half hours. Since it was a private room, we stayed with her until it was finished. This was the least I could do to complete the cycle of life for my dog. From the day I first carried her out of the pet store in my arms, I would carry her ashes out in my arms. There is no way I would leave her there by herself. After arriving home, we sat out on the back patio, just staring into space. I posted the news of St. Clair's passing on Facebook and watched all of the condolences posted on my page.

My cousin called and I told her that I wished St. Clair would send a message so I would know that she was okay. For some reason, our mail didn't come that day until 7:30 p.m. in the evening. My partner went to retrieve it, and when he returned, he held up one of the many dog catalogs we receive, this one with a photo of an Airedale on the front with, "Best Dog Ever" imprinted on his collar. What better sign!

The following Sunday on the car ride home from our cottage, I looked into the sky wondering about St. Clair. I desperately wanted some kind of sign from her again. It came, in the form of a pure, white feather. Walking up to the side gate of our yard, I saw a white feather perfectly placed in my path. Having read extensively about the afterlife, I learned about signs we might receive from our deceased loved ones. Feathers, especially white ones, hold special significance. I found credibility in the explanations and believe these feathers provide reassurance that our loved ones are still near and watching over us. For me, finding feathers reinforces my ongoing connection with St. Clair. Since her death, I have found countless feathers of all shapes, sizes, and colors and in the most unexpected places.

I believe that St. Clair communicated with me in two significant ways while on a business trip in Florida. The first communication occurred as I got out of my rental car and turned to walk toward my destination. In that moment, a white truck passed by with the name "St. Clair's Furniture" written on the side. On my return flight home, I decided to watch a popular television program, and this is where the second, unexpected sign occurred. Because of my interest in the arts, I enjoy watching the credits that appear at the end of every episode. Much to my surprise and delight, the name "Julie St. Clair" rolled by on the screen. I watched the very next episode of that show, paying close attention to the credits, and that name did not reappear.

Exactly one week after St. Clair's death, the priest at my church conducted a small remembrance service for her. He included a few readings from the Bible about animals and blessed St. Clair's urn in the process. In the weeks that followed, I somehow made it through each day, but nothing held my interest. I laughed when it was appropriate and did what I needed at work, but at home, I spent a lot of time crying and preferred to be alone. I was wracked with guilt that I raised my voice at my sweet dog. I was filled with regret and was unable to forgive myself. Why did I go to those appointments, when I could see she wasn't doing well? Why of all mornings did I make that choice? I couldn't have known that this would be her final morning with us nor how fast she was going downhill with no possible chance of recovery. But I still felt horrible. Instead of going to my appointments, I should have taken her to the emergency vet *immediately*. As I look back, I've learned that whether I had taken her in the morning or the afternoon, the outcome would have been the same.

Everyone in my workplace was incredibly kind and supportive. My boss let me take time off without having to use vacation days. When I returned to work, my co-workers were very kind and sympathetic if I cried at my desk. Much to my amazement, I received more condolence cards for St. Clair than I had received after the death of my father. Many of the cards had lovely verses and personal notes written inside. As the months passed, I could occasionally talk about my dog without crying. However, it didn't take much for a few droplets to turn into a major stream.

I started to question if my feelings were justified. Grieving my Dad's death had been so different. With a human being, you might get to speak with them before the end *and* you receive a response. If you're lucky you might also get to sort out differences and even mend a fence or two. With animals, our love is expressed in far simpler, less complicated ways — which is why we love them so intensely. I don't have kids, so St. Clair was essentially my child. She depended on me for everything and was the first priority in my life.

Since my sadness lasted a lot longer than I expected, I decided to look for a support group. I found Beyond the Paw Print Pet Loss Support Group through an online search, promptly sent an email, and received a response from the founder, Dr. Micky Golden Moore. We corresponded several times, which helped me find some comfort before my first meeting.

Once I attended the group in person, I was shocked, yet in a way, comforted that I wasn't the only one struggling with my loss. Hearing other stories validated my own. I didn't always leave happy, however, a few days later I seemed to feel a bit better. The emotional release, as well as the realization that I wasn't going crazy, was liberating. My tears and grief were acknowledged. I found that sharing my story in the group was better than internalizing all of my feelings.

One important conclusion I've reached by attending BTPP meetings and reading materials on grief is that you never *get over it.*

This is my new normal. That's why it's called a journey, but one that doesn't end. The journey merely changes shape as we reach a new level of inner growth and understanding. I've learned not to try to push my feelings aside but acknowledge and work with them. I've adjusted to a new way of life and have learned to accept my loss.

So why would anyone want to go on this journey? *Because we have an unlimited capacity for love.* The unconditional love we receive from an animal far exceeds anything material and provides the sweetest kind of comfort, especially to those living alone, as I had been for so long. My dog was my constant sidekick, and a great friend to me in my single days.

We marked the one-year anniversary of St. Clair's death, on July 31, 2018. I knew all of this would be hard, but I didn't know quite *how* hard. There's no other way to get around death, and grief, but to go through it. I've gone about my daily life with routines that used to involve St. Clair — like taking a vacation, celebrating a birthday (hers and mine), Christmas, or the New Year. Doing them alone has hit me hard, especially returning home to an empty house. Walking into a pet store knowing I wasn't there to buy something for St. Clair was painful. Maybe every year will be hard. Maybe it will get easier. Only time will tell.

About three months after St. Clair's passing, I had a memorial tattoo inscribed on my right forearm. I always wanted a tattoo, but didn't know what shape it would take. What better way to memorialize my beloved dog? I also found an old dog tag with her name on it which I now wear on a chain around my neck. I've spent time as a volunteer for an established animal organization and have donated food and other items to local shelters. My backyard has a section with a special sign that reads, "St. Clair's Memorial Garden." She enjoyed playing and relaxing in that part of the garden and had once munched on the Hosta plants that grew there.

I also received what some people might consider an unusual gift. A friend bought me a session with an animal communicator, a person who specializes in receiving messages from beloved animals who have died. Some might react with skepticism or question what would lead me to connect with someone like this. Initially, I was a bit skeptical too. However, I found tremendous comfort from my session and am now very open to those who may possess this special gift.

The communicator said that St. Clair was showing her a red rose. "To me, this means ultimate sacrifice, unconditional love and secrets shared," the communicator said. "I feel this is reflective of your relationship." What better sign could I have possibly received? I was amazed by this person's words. The only people who knew about the red rose that I'd placed in her paws at the crematorium were my partner and myself. During our reading, the communicator mentioned other special attributes and activities that confirmed my belief that she was accurately describing my very own St. Clair. This is a gift I will treasure forever.

As I reflect on the past year, I was that person who walked out of the vet's office saying through my tears, "I will never get another dog!" vowing not to put myself through this pain again. My need to love though has outweighed this vow, made in the midst of raw grief. But was I truly ready to adopt? It had not even been a year when I started to feel the desire to bring another dog into our lives. I kept in contact with an Airedale rescue organization, and they actively searched for a dog on my behalf. We are now the proud owners of a twenty-month-old rescued Airedale named Murphy. He's the total opposite of St. Clair in every way.

I didn't automatically feel, to be honest, that Murphy was the "one" when I first met him. But I began to seriously consider adopting him after I learned that he needed to be re-homed; Murphy had been a "return to breeder"— twice, by the same family — at five and six months old because of aggression issues. The problem wasn't readily apparent during our visits, although it surfaced shortly after we brought him home. It turns out he's very possessive of me and doesn't like others to get in close proximity. Through the assistance of animal behaviorists, training classes, and maturity, Murphy has grown out of this behavior. Having a bodyguard always sounded like a fun idea, I just never knew it would come in the form of an Airedale!

Even though I've opened my heart to Murphy, I still feel St. Clair's gentle tug with every fiber of my being. I believe we all have an unlimited capacity to love. I arrived at this conclusion through personal experience. Time, patience, and the grieving process have revealed that my heart has room for both Murphy and St. Clair.

The discovery that Murphy could help me through my sadness over losing St. Clair has been an unexpected gift. Without him, I might still be wallowing in my grief. Murphy loves to play — is downright rowdy at times — and is just full of life. I call him my Velcro Boy: He sticks to my side constantly. No matter where I am in our home, he's right next to me, leaning against me. I love this little fellow.

OTTER & DAKOTA

STORY TWO

My Reason and Purpose

By Kate

I HAD JUST GRADUATED FROM COLLEGE with a degree in zoology, and, like most people my age, was looking for my dream job. Given that my home state of Michigan wasn't exactly awash in zookeeper positions, I realized quickly that I might need a Plan B. Despite being surrounded by our own bodies of water — numerous lakes and streams, it isn't exactly home to marine mammals. I loved animals and I knew for certain that I wanted to dedicate my life to them.

The next best thing was to try for a position at a nearby canine training and daycare center. I was granted an interview and to my delight, got the job. It was here, amidst oodles of puppies of all different ages and breeds, that I met and fell in love with two Yellow Labradors, Otter and Dakota, who changed my life forever. Of all the animals in my care at the training and daycare center, these two captured my heart.

Dakota was the elder one, a little more mature, wiser, and much more stoic. He had an old soul yet loved without boundaries. His yellow fur was wavy, thick, and inviting to the touch. His slightly curved tail was always in motion. Never did we interact when there was not a kiss from Dakota. Being with him was like being with my best friend; you knew you were loved and protected.

Otter was younger, a ball of yellow fur with brown eyes that could melt the coldest of hearts. He was the kind of puppy that would crawl on top of you and kiss you all over while his tail wagged at the speed of light causing his plump little body to quiver with excitement.

Otter and Dakota were the reason I actually enjoyed getting up at the crack of dawn to rush to my job. They were the reason that work seemed like play. They were always the highlight of my day and grew to be the same in my life. Otter and Dakota also became my project. I poured everything I learned about obedience training into them, wanting them to be the very best, well-behaved dogs for their owner. They were perfect students. The more I learned, the more I gave them.

As it turned out, their owner, Ross needed a dog sitter. I was hired and the extra time I spent with Otter and Dakota allowed us to bond even further. They knew what I wanted before I could say the words and appeared to anticipate my needs.

Everywhere we went, everyone wanted an Otter and Dakota. I was so proud of them. They brought out the best in me and I was elated to think that I was partially responsible for their wonderful dispositions. During the months that I worked with these two, another relationship developed that changed the course of my entire life. Ross became an even closer friend, then my boyfriend, which produced a marriage proposal and a wedding! We often joke that I fell in love with Otter and Dakota first.

How could life get any better? I had the best husband, the best dogs, and a family anyone would want. I also had the best job. With a deep interest in the care and well-being of animals, I returned to school and became a licensed veterinary technician. After graduation, I found my dream job at the same veterinary hospital where Otter and Dakota had been patients. They were selfless and loving dogs, easily adapting to life with the arrival of two babies, a Basset Hound, and a cat. Never once did they lose their passion to play, love, and protect. The speed at which they ran after each other in the yard was like watching wild horses, and the love they felt for one another was expressed best during nap time; they always had to be touching.

As the years progressed, so did the wear and tear of time on Otter and Dakota. Otter's back had started giving him problems and surgery was not an option. With any type of movement, his spinal discs could easily slip out of place, causing compression on his nerves. Keeping him comfortable was all we could manage when he had flare-ups. His body, although still appearing to be its sleek self, could no longer charge through the yard as quickly and seamlessly as it once did. The lifelong joke of his name, Otter, didn't always apply: Our dog didn't actually like water, or to swim, at all.

Each morning we wondered if Otter was going to have a good day, or if it would be another one filled with debilitating back pain. As a family, we were saddened to see his hesitation in tackling stairs. We had frequent discussions about "when and how" we would say goodbye. The time was fast approaching, and we recognized the most loving action would take him away from us yet release him from his suffering and pain. I'm a trained veterinary technician and euthanasia comes with the territory. I had loved and lost many of my own special childhood pets. But this was Otter and he was my bright star. His face, those brown eyes and sweet, fun-loving personality were soon to be gone. I realized that only days remained.

There was a heavy feeling in our household knowing that our sweet dog would be leaving us soon. One day, in the midst of this crisis, Ross called me from outside. There was a sense of urgency in his voice, so I stopped what I was doing and rushed to see what was happening. I ran to find Dakota on the ground, lifeless. He had been perfectly fine earlier, meeting me with his trademark friendly tail wag and kiss. My brain went into work mode, but the emotional side of me realized that this was serious. Otter was ill, not Dakota. How could this be happening?

I tried to understand as I rushed him to the veterinary hospital. We soon learned that Dakota was bleeding internally at such a rapid rate that even blood transfusions wouldn't save him. The group of vets and technicians worked tirelessly to come up with answers, while Dakota became weaker from the blood loss. The disease process was taking over his body, time was running out, and a decision had to be made. I understood that I was losing Dakota, my guardian, my confidant, my anchor, my hero. With his family surrounding him, now very weak, and tired, Dakota was euthanized. He looked so peaceful and I knew that he was running freely over the rainbow bridge.

In the days that followed, Ross and I were in a state of disbelief, trying to explain to our children what happened and answer the questions that only innocent minds ask: "Where is Dakota? What happened to Dakota? Isn't Otter sick?" The hard part was that I had no answers. How could I explain to my children the twisted turn of events that had just taken place?

Four days later, I heard a horrible noise. It can only be described as a shrill screaming, and it was coming from Otter. Again, as I had four days earlier, I ran outside, only this time to find Otter curled around himself and crying out loud in pain while trying to walk to me. I thought, no way, not now. Not this soon after losing Dakota. My family was already devastated, and even though we had just talked about Otter and how we would help him when his time came, we were emotionally unprepared.

I was able to position him on a blanket in our back yard and made him comfortable until the veterinarian arrived. I couldn't move him, which was maybe to my benefit, since I couldn't imagine walking through the doors where we'd been with Dakota just four days earlier. Gone were the days of the goofy running and jumping motions he did that made me think of him as a reindeer taking flight. With the sun on his face and our family gathered around again, we said goodbye to Otter. He too was at peace and out of pain. I hoped more than anything that he was now playing chase with his brother, running and jumping with endless joy, together over the rainbow bridge.

In no time at all, I had lost my two best friends. I had also lost my ability to reason. I had lost my soul. I even felt like I had lost my mind. My nights were sleepless since I was plagued with nightmares. Even though friends and family were there with support, as were my Basset Hound and cat, I was beyond devastated. I had never felt such a crippling pain and had never felt so alone. Everyone's life just kept going, while I had a hard time breathing. I didn't go back to work. I didn't want to. I had no desire to work with any other animals considering I couldn't even save my own. I simply went through the motions each day and night but felt numb.

After an internet search on pet bereavement, I found Dr. Micky Golden Moore and Beyond the Paw Print. I hoped that this group might help me make sense of the passing of Otter and Dakota. Through the meetings, I felt a shift, from pain to purpose. I was able to share my grief, my anger, and my sadness, in confidence with people who understood. Everyone there was in the same position, yet in different parts of their journey—which gave me hope. BTPP became my safe haven and the place where I found balance.

With Micky's guidance, I saw a light through my darkest days. BTPP helped me rediscover my direction. I began to feel an energy inside that soon turned into a fiery passion. I wanted to learn everything I could about pet bereavement and how to help make a difference. I was determined to help others through the same debilitating grief, never wanting anyone to feel they were alone in their journey. I earned a certificate in pet bereavement counseling through an online course offered by The Association for Pet Loss and Bereavement. The program was excellent. In addition, I listened and learned from the attendees at the BTPP meetings. I found a niche for myself at the veterinary clinic where I worked; reaching out to clients in need of grief support. I began to find meaning again.

With encouragement from Micky, I started my own pet bereavement group, and called it Pathway to Peace. I felt grateful that I could provide support for others on their path to find peace in a world without their beloved pet. To this day, I can honestly say I learned more from my attendees than they learned from me. It was I who was truly given a gift. I listened as stories were shared, dried the largest of tears, and held each special memento close to my heart. I shared a part of their joy and happiness as well as provided comfort as they grieved.

The clients who came to me initially distraught with grief soon became close friends, and their gratitude is boundless. I love knowing that Pathway to Peace made a difference, connecting with others in a world where communication is more often made through a touch screen than a human touch. Thank you, Otter and Dakota. Thank you for giving me the best years of my life. Thank you for teaching me how to support others when they are at their most vulnerable.

As I enter my twentieth year as a licensed veterinary technician, I am grateful for all that I have learned about love, loss, and healing. My personal journey has enabled me to connect in a deeper, more meaningful way with our clients. I love any and all opportunities to support others who may be grieving the loss of a beloved companion. Otter and Dakota were my life, my reason, my purpose. I made a choice to honor them by helping others regain their purpose. I pay tribute to their memory in the way they would have wanted; by opening my heart to another.

About three months after we said goodbye to Otter and Dakota, my husband Ross came home and told me about a litter of Yellow Lab puppies that were for sale at a pheasant farm nearby. "Let's go!" I said. Off we went and I soon found myself on the floor with close to ten puppies! Although all of them were adorable, there was something special about one little pup. He was inquisitive, lovable and fought his way through the others to get my attention. The instant connection was there. We named him Walter. In him, I see my beloved dogs. I see the playfulness of Otter and the fierce loyalty of Dakota. Most of all, I have been able to see love again. Although your time came to an end my sweet Otter and Dakota, the bright light in your souls lives on.

KNUCKLEHEAD & CONNER

STORY THREE

Cats Have Staff

By Diana

"DOGS HAVE OWNERS AND CATS HAVE STAFF." It's a saying I soon learned when we rescued a six-week-old tuxedo kitty, the runt of a litter born in my parents' garage. On that day in 1980, I became a loyal "cat servant." Knucklehead was one of five kittens in the litter of a stray female whom my mom had been feeding and eventually took into her home. My husband decided, with my support, to adopt the "little runt," as he called him. Knucklehead was a beautiful black and white, short-haired cat, and only six weeks old at that point. I couldn't think of a name for him for the longest time, until one day he was hanging out with me while I was painting. "You little knucklehead!" I said as he walked across a newly finished shelf. The name just stuck and suited him perfectly. He was my little Knucklehead, for life.

And what a life it was. I hadn't grown up with pets, and it wasn't until I married that I would know the joy of pet parenthood. My husband, Tony, grew up with cats, dogs, and a rooster. Knucklehead was our first rescue. We later found ChiChi in Tony's parent's backyard, and then Conner in the streets in Detroit.

Everyone loved Knucklehead and his quirky personality. You wouldn't dare have French fries without making sure he had a few to nibble on. At night, I was delighted that he would sleep soundly on my chest — tuckered out from all his activities. Knucklehead loved to play fetch with just about anything. Although he was neutered, our boy had a somewhat perverse affection for white athletic socks. "Knucklehead, you had better not bring any baby socks home!" my husband would say. Everybody loved our boy. He was never hesitant to join the party and would take advantage of any open seat. I have never had another cat like my first baby.

At about the age of fourteen, I noticed that Knucklehead had begun losing weight, although he was eating well at the time. I made an appointment with our veterinarian, where Knucklehead received a thorough exam and blood work. Soon after, our vet diagnosed him with an overactive thyroid. The doctor explained that the illness wasn't unusual for older cats, and his treatment plan included an oral medication dispensed daily. Over the next four years, we followed this regimen and saw the doctor on several occasions. In his eighteenth year though, Knucklehead's body just started to give out. One final hospitalization, with additional treatment, did not improve his condition. We were told to continue his medication and shower him with love. Providing tenderness and affection was the easy part. As Knucklehead became more detached from me and lost more weight, we knew it wouldn't be long.

One night, instead of sleeping with us, Knucklehead left our bedroom and went to the basement. I've heard so often that animals want to be alone in death, and it held true here: Knucklehead crossed the rainbow bridge in our basement and Tony found him the next morning. Telling me my boy had died during the night was the hardest thing Tony ever had to do. Although that was nineteen years ago, I still cry and continue to feel guilty when I think that he died alone and not in our loving arms. I do have faith though that Knucklehead knew how much we loved him.

We had found Conner only four years after adopting Knucklehead. I was working at the customer service office of a utility company in Detroit and was visiting one of our newer locations one day when a little black kitten walked through an open door. The office supervisor told me that the kitten kept showing up every day, and every day the supervisor would remove him from the premises. While there, I made some telephone calls at a desk and the sweet black kitten jumped on my lap. None of the workers were interested in taking him home, but I was. The kitten was so beautiful, and just melted my heart. I called my husband to speak to him about it.

"We already have two cats — what's one more??" "Well," he replied dryly, "I would advise against bringing another cat home." We ended our call and I continued to work, while the kitty continued to sit on my lap. When it was time to leave, I decided that I couldn't abandon this little beauty; he would surely meet an early demise out there on his own. Against Tony's advice, I put him in a box and took him with me. As I walked through the front door, Tony was there expectantly. "I hope there isn't a cat in that box," he said. He knew there was.

That was the beginning of our relationship with Conner, who was only twelve weeks old at the time. Like Knucklehead, Conner was very affectionate, loved to be with us, and loved to sleep on my chest or at least nearby. After only a few days, Conner was sleeping under the covers near my feet. One night, I tried to move him, but he was as stiff as a board. I thought he was dead! I yelled for Tony, which woke Conner up. He was in a sleep stupor, something we realized, as time went by, was typical for him; saying he was a sound sleeper was an understatement. Conner and Knucklehead bonded quickly, and there was nothing he enjoyed more than snuggling with his buddy in their basket in front of the fireplace.

Our Conner was prone to showing his love in other ways,

like the time he laid a mouse on my chest in the middle of the night. There I was, sleeping peacefully, when he jumped on the bed and dropped something squarely on my chest. Since I know cats to be hunters, my first thought was, "There had better not be a mouse on my chest!" Perhaps this was a pet owner's intuition. Sure enough, I opened my eyes and there was a mouse and Conner, and the mouse was still alive. I screamed for Tony. Both the animals and Tony took off, all chasing each other. As I remained under the covers, I could hear Tony and Conner wrestling the frightened rodent. When the mouse smackdown came to an end, the score was Tony and Conner 1, Mouse, zero. We all went back to our corners and, thankfully, retired for the night.

Tony often said he was glad I rescued Conner, despite his reluctance, which was music to my ears. Just after Knucklehead died, we found that Conner was acting strangely. We thought it was that he missed Knucklehead and had a broken heart. How naive of us to believe that animals don't grieve. Conner was Knucklehead's best friend. After a few days of not eating and drinking properly, he was only getting worse. We brought him promptly to our veterinarian: Conner was in kidney failure. We started fluid treatments to keep him hydrated. Initially, the treatment appeared helpful, but only three weeks later, while I was at a conference and Tony was at work, my mom, who came to our home to check on Conner, found him dead in our kitchen.

Tony phoned and told me the devastating news. I was crushed. Processing the experience was impossible, especially since I was away and needed to maintain my composure while in a business setting. Instead of offering support, my colleagues appeared disgusted by it all, and couldn't understand my grief. If Conner had been a dog, the reaction probably would have been very different. Out of fifteen people at the meetings, only one man approached me to express his condolences. It was a horrible two days before I could finally go home and openly express my grief with my husband and my parents.

Our hearts were broken after losing these two very special kitties who had been a part of our lives for so long. Knucklehead and

Conner were very close, and I'm certain that Conner died from grief over the loss of his best friend. My husband and I have suffered the loss of grandparents and parents but none of our losses have seemed so great as the loss of these two very special fur babies.

Those who have not been touched by the soft paw of an animal don't realize the deep love that can exist between a human being and their pet. This lack of understanding is most apparent when our beloved pets pass on. When a human being dies, most companies think nothing of providing bereavement time. Friends send sympathy cards and people are empathetic. When a beloved pet dies, one is expected to immediately jump back into work and life. People are forced to grieve in isolation, fearing rejection or ridicule over being able to express their true emotions.

Grief is not the only emotion pet lovers experience. All too often, guilt is associated with a pet's death too. Questions that dominate our thoughts adding further stress may include, "Did I do everything I could?" or "Why didn't I take action sooner?" I've often wished that Knucklehead and Conner could have talked to us, to warn us, to tell us how they felt in their final moments. These lingering feelings left me wanting to do something significant in their memory.

In 2010, my friend Gina, a veterinary technician, told me about the fate of injured and ill stray animals who are brought into veterinary hospitals by good Samaritans. Most often the good Samaritan can't keep the animal or afford to pay their medical needs. It was then that we decided that we could make a difference by raising money to fund medical treatment for abandoned and stray animals. That was the beginning of, *4 Paws 1 Heart*. One of the ways people learn about our organization are through guest speaking opportunities.

When I was asked to make a presentation about my organization to Micky's group, I was happy to connect with her and meet the attendees of the group. As the facilitator, Micky leads the meeting with compassion and care for each attendee. One significant outcome of the meeting is that attendees learn that their grief is legitimate. The meetings also provide a safe, confidential outlet for sharing feelings of loss *and* love. Just voicing one's emotions, in the open, can be very cathartic for those present, who learn they are not alone, and that their grief is recognized. I saw that I was very fortunate to have the support system of my husband, my parents, and my sister, who loved my cats and accepted the overwhelming grief I experienced when it came time to say goodbye. Not everyone is so lucky.

In my work with *4 Paws 1 Heart*, I often find myself in the position of helping someone in their grieving over a lost pet, or a rescue they weren't able to save. Everyone deals with grief in their own way. Many people never adopt or rescue again because they can't face the idea of yet another heartbreaking loss. I encourage people to honor their loved one by saving another. There are millions of stray and abandoned animals in need of loving homes. There's no better way to say thank you for the love they so generously gave.

My husband and I knew that the only way to say thank you and to honor the unconditional love we were so lucky to have received from Knucklehead and Conner was to promptly save two more cats. That's what we did and continue to do today. We are now the proud servants of three rescue cats, all tuxedos: Sophia, twelve; Nunzio, eleven; and Luigi, nine, my baby.

I still find myself, like any pet parent, occasionally referring to one of our current family members as Knucklehead or Conner. My boys will always be in my heart. They are the reason I continue to save as many animals as possible and the reason I believe so strongly in spay/neuter. As much as I love our current family, no one can ever replace Knucklehead and Conner. They will be in my heart forever. Sometimes, during the night, I think I can feel Knucklehead or Conner jumping on the bed. I'm comforted by their presence and have confidence that their spirits will always live on. I'm sure they'll be waiting at the Rainbow Bridge for me on the day I start my next journey.

LINCOLN

STORY FOUR

Super Dog

By Ian

THE BAD NEWS FIRST: Your dog is *not* the best dog in the world. I'm sorry to tell you this. He or she may be the second best in the world, maybe tied for ninth, or the 23rd best dog, but not number one. I know this because for over fifteen years I was lucky enough to have had the best dog in the world, and his name was Lincoln.

As I reflect on the life and loss of Lincoln, it's occurred to me that sometimes you don't recognize the most momentous times of your life. They blend in with the hundreds of other encounters, decisions, and events that occur through time. That can be said of the day I met Lincoln, one that was loaded with meaning and in the end, far more than I ever realized.

I can picture the day so clearly. It was a beautiful June evening in northeast Ohio, and I had just arrived home from work. As I opened my car door, there he was, a jubilant puppy jumping onto my lap and licking my face. My then-wife had made no mention of getting a dog, or even of wanting one. She was a schoolteacher, and with the summer off, thought that would be the perfect time to bring a new furry friend into our home. She had gone to our local dog pound that morning and spotted Lincoln, a mix of Black Labrador and Golden Retriever. His head was emblazoned with one small white spot, like a streak of white paint he'd accidentally rubbed against in the course of snooping somewhere he didn't belong. That playful mark drew her to Lincoln out of a room full of long-faced compatriots, all waiting for their savior.

I should note that my present wife, Tina, often wonders why I harbor no anger towards my ex-wife. The reason is simple: She brought Lincoln into my life. As a child, my friends had posters of NFL and NBA players in their rooms. I had one of Honest Abe, our sixteenth president and my idol. Lincoln is the name of one of the greatest Americans, and one I had to bestow on my beloved dog. As first-time dog parents, we purchased all the usual items, including a cage for our new friend to sleep in on his first night with us. During the course of the evening, Lincoln softly howled at the utter loneliness and isolation. I just couldn't bear it. I let him out and allowed him to sleep on our bed. He'd never be put in that cage again.

Lincoln and I bonded immediately, and I became his favorite. When we went for walks, I took him off the leash in the fields across from our condominium. Lincoln would constantly look back to make sure I was there. If I would ever sneak away, he would take off at a gallop to find me. Sometimes if my wife was walking him, I'd climb a tree in the field and watch from above as he caught the first hint of my scent. He'd race around until he narrowed the search to that tree and would then race in circles below, unable to fathom that I could be up above staring down. It was all good fun.

As the years went by, Lincoln became a huge fan of pillows. He found them far more comfortable than he did laying his head at the bottom of the bed. If I let him out in the middle of the night, Lincoln would patiently wait while I wiped his paws, but would then race me to the bed for the coveted comfy pillow. If he won, he'd sheepishly look at me as I would joke with him by curling up at the bottom of the bed. One night he woke me for what I presumed was a signal that he needed to go outside. I pulled open the sliding glass door and waited for him to walk onto the porch. A few seconds later, I realized he had run back to the bed and taken my spot on the pillow again — a total fake out!

My vet called him Super Dog. Cancer, hip dysplasia, foreign object removal from the stomach, torn ACL — nothing stopped Lincoln, until one thing did; a condition called Mega-Esophagus. Unable to keep food down, he would aspirate it into his lungs, which in turn led to pneumonia. Lincoln had weathered the first bout in June 2011. A trip to the veterinary school at Michigan State University that fall for further testing yielded no cure. Despite this sad news, we minimized the effects of the disease through diet and changes to his feeding process, and for the time being Lincoln returned to near normal.

One year later, his breathing started to become labored again, and I took him to the emergency clinic in the middle of the night. It was a second bout of pneumonia. Everything felt different this time. After so many trips through the years to different vets, this one didn't have that optimistic tenor, that Super Dog would pull through. Lincoln had to stay in the hospital since he needed to be put on oxygen; I visited him every night after work. The vet told me that they had to begin weaning him off the oxygen, but I could see that he still needed it. After three days, the hospital staff said it would be alright to take him home. When he came out of the room, he was walking very slowly and dragging his tail.

The next ten days were rough. Lincoln was very lethargic and had almost no appetite from the Mega-Esophagus condition. There were many days he would throw up what I fed him. On his last night, I woke to him throwing up slightly along with labored breathing. I laid with him on the floor to comfort him. In the morning, I took him outside. He ate a meatball with his medicine and then rested on a pile of blankets that we had set up in the basement. I leaned down and patted him on the head and said what I had said to him every time I left the house for the last fifteen years: "I'll be back."

At 3:13 in the afternoon on October 18, Tina called crying and told me she was rushing him to the vet. He had been at the bottom of the stairs waiting for help when she got home, and his breathing was very labored. She slowly led him to the door, and he walked about 30 feet and collapsed onto the ground. She drove the van around to the backyard and lifted him in with help from her son, driving as fast as she could to the emergency clinic. By the time I got there, he was gone. The vet told me that in the end it was the pneumonia that actually caused his death.

Writing those words almost six years later and picturing him at the bottom of the stairs waiting for someone to come home and help him fills me with a sadness that I will not even attempt to describe. I went to work the next day, and gratefully people left me alone. I was functioning but numb for weeks. I tried to keep my grief hidden around Tina as she too was distraught, but I was worse. She kept telling me that I should talk to someone. I refused at first. As a man in his forties, the thought of sitting around telling strangers how sad I was about my dog being gone smacked of self-pity and misplaced priorities in a world with so many other problems. The passage of time wasn't helping either. I sensed Tina's growing frustration, so I relented. She had done the research and talked with Dr. Micky Golden Moore, the founder of Beyond the Paw Print Pet Loss Support Group, and thought it was the best option.

Micky facilitates her meetings guided by the needs of those present. Returning attendees — or veterans, as I like to call them — start the meeting by sharing their stories or updates. This gives newcomers time to get oriented with the group and learn from the veterans' experiences. On that first night, those who spoke before me kept their emotions in check. When it was my turn, I was OK for a while but then became a basket case. I was embarrassed, but being with people who understood and supported me was exactly what I wanted at that time. A recurring theme at the meetings was that many of our peers don't understand how anyone could become so attached to a pet. It was a waste of time confiding in unsympathetic people, the analogy being you don't go to a hardware store to buy bread. My situation was slightly different. My friends and family knew all too well how much Lincoln meant to me. In fact, long before his passing, they said they wouldn't want to be around the day that he would leave this world, knowing it wouldn't be pretty. Somehow, I found it easier to talk about Lincoln and my grief with Micky's group once a month than to my inner circle.

Discussing Lincoln at BTPP helped me realize that there were two prongs to the core of my sadness: One was simply that of losing a truly remarkable companion that I had planned my day around for fifteen years. I took proactive steps to help manage this loss. First, I tried to have a certain time every day to think about him. If I felt my mind wandering to thoughts of Lincoln before my designated daily time, I told myself that "Lincoln Time" was coming up.

Second, was the passage of time itself. Lincoln was fifteen and a half years old when he died. He was a big dog, 70 pounds at his peak. Had he survived the second bout of pneumonia it is unlikely he would have had another year with me regardless of what had happened medically. Third, as the one-year anniversary of his death came and went, I understood that despite my wanting another year with him, it would have ended at some point. I had to start appreciating the amazing times we'd shared and not dwell on Lincoln's not being with me anymore.

The other prong of my grief was more insidious: It was guilt. Two hours after Lincoln passed, I began writing down all the things that I could have done differently, that would have prevented his loss. I tweaked, combined, and modified them and ended up with six distinct acts that caused him to go downhill. I thought about these six distinct acts for months and discussed them at BTPP, as well as with my friends and family. "What if I . . . If only . . . I should have . . . Why didn't I… I could have… I should have…" A constant loop of guilt. Everyone was patient with me: They told me that it was just his time. Only by thinking through each of these six distinct acts, and reviewing what I knew and could observe that horrible day, was I able to reconcile my feelings. As I attended monthly meetings, eventually, I became one of those "veterans" that could talk about their pet with love and not with tears.

Despite all the pain I endured, I was able to take one final step in my healing. One of the veteran BTPP attendees, Karen, brought photos of her past and present Golden Retrievers, Scout and Casey, to the meetings. They were beautiful dogs with kind, bright eyes and wide doggie smiles. I would often tell Tina that I did not want another dog, but if I ever did, it would be a Golden. It's been stressed in the BTPP meetings that getting a new pet was a very personal decision and that it may or may not help the grieving process.

On January 31, 2014, that decision was made for me. I came home to Tina standing by the door looking timid, holding a wiggling towel on her shoulder. "What did you do?" I asked repeatedly. She seemed nervous and looked as though she might start to cry. Tina had even bought the puppy name tags. Reagan, an eight-week-old Golden Retriever, was now part of our family. Tina, accustomed to sleep deprivation after having been a single mom raising two kids, quickly realized what a perfect dog Lincoln had been. Reagan was yet another baby, a puppy, which meant he would be waking us up often, always getting into trouble, always chewing, unlike Lincoln who possessed extraordinary calmness.

Reagan has helped me with Lincoln's loss in that I've been able to recognize their differences. Reagan is a wonderful dog, with every attribute you'd expect from a Golden Retriever, but he doesn't possess Lincoln's loyalty. Don't get me wrong, there's nothing wrong with that. It just makes Lincoln's memory even more special. Dog owners know the drill: You come home from work, the dog is standing by the spouse who's cooking, the dog pivots his head back and forth between the food and the newly arrived owner who wants to bend over and scratch his ears. Most dogs though, including Reagan, stay with the food.

Lincoln? He always appeared happy for me to arrive home. He would run toward me and greet me, even if only for a moment before returning stove side. This was our daily routine. Here was someone who brought me out of myself, by his sheer unadulterated joy at my presence. He loved life and he loved me. Whenever we were together, my spirits lifted. Lincoln had a soul, a loving, caring, selfless soul.

My final thought about losing Lincoln, and what, if anything, others can gain from my experience, comes from two issues often raised at BTPP meetings. I would listen as newcomers beat themselves up for not being there at the end to provide final comfort, and then hear other newcomers express guilt over being there at the end and not being able to help. These are two sides of the same coin, both with a concern that their beloved companion left this world with either a feeling of loneliness or confusion.

Neither is true. There is no "better place" for you to be at the end. After years of bestowing on your pet all the characteristics, intelligence, and emotions that any sentient human possesses, it's important for you to know the following: They knew how much you loved them. Believe that they were not second-guessing your whereabouts or intentions. Hold close to your heart the love you gave your pet throughout their entire life. When the end came, they were thinking the same.

MAISY

STORY FIVE

My Sweet Shadow

By Mary Ellen

IN MY PET-OWNING LIFE, I have had a charming cast of four-legged friends. There was Cookie, the Dalmatian, a.k.a., Cookie Monster; Brandy, our laid-back Golden Retriever who served as both dog and rug; and Casper, a Chow mix, who liked to jump six-foot fences. Memories of each hold a significant place in my heart and life. This story is about Maisy, my gentle soul, who was and always will be, top dog in my heart.

Before Maisy came into our lives, we were dog-less, again. A time without a dog, as all owners know, is one where there's a void, without the flurry of daily tail wagging or the panting face and toothy grin meeting you at the door. Rescue, to me, was the only thing that would help change that. So many pets need homes where they can be loved and give love. Our family agreed the time was right and I started an earnest search to fill our home again with that unconditional love.

I first saw Maisy, who was then named Marla, on a local rescue website. She was a six-week-old terrier mix with white and tan markings. She appeared so cute in her picture. The next day I decided we needed to pay Marla a visit. I picked up my son from kindergarten and off we went to the rescue's Detroit location to try to meet her. I asked to see Marla, and when directed to the room where the dogs were kept, I spotted her immediately. She was so much cuter in person! Her scent and the softness of her fur, it was love at first sight! I held Marla in my arms and carried her into the social room. She tugged at a leash toy and looked at me with the sweetest eyes. That was it: She would become the newest member of the family!

My son's excitement was also evident. He wanted her as much as I did. We grabbed Marla's tag from her cage and went to the adoption desk. For the moment though, our joy had to be put on hold. A notation on the tag said Marla was not to be adopted into a home with children under the age of six. My son quickly told the adoption agent that he would be very careful with her, and that he was almost six. We all smiled, knowing then and there that this puppy was going home with us.

My husband and daughter had yet to meet Marla, but we were all in agreement that she needed a new name. I liked Daisy but that quickly got shot down. Many other names were mentioned, but we couldn't decide. Finally, someone said "Maisy!" It sounded like Daisy, but the kids liked it better. Maisy it was.

We had to wait three days to bring our new dog home since she needed to be spayed. In the meantime, we bought a crate, dog dish, food and toys so we would be fully prepared for her arrival. Finally, the big day had arrived. My son and daughter were at after-school day care and couldn't wait to see their new puppy. When he picked them up, my husband was holding Maisy in a little cardboard box on his lap. The kids ran out to the car, excited beyond belief. Welcome Maisy!!

We soon got to know our new puppy, and she, us, which included learning her many special habits. Some dogs chase rabbits and squirrels, our Maisy chased planes. She would look up in the sky and wait for a plane to fly overhead. Immediately, she would start barking and running wildly back and forth, doing circles in the yard. This happened repeatedly. Eventually, she'd succumb to her thirst and paw at the door to get in, drinking heartily from her water bowl. After she had enough water, Maisy would collapse on the cold kitchen tile. After a brief nap, the pawing at the door would start anew for another trip back outside for more fun.

Pawing or scratching, we soon discovered, was one of Maisy's prime methods of communication. She would paw at the couch, the wall, the kitchen cabinets, the door or even me. Her actions signaled her need to go outside, or that she was bored, wanted treats, a cuddle — any or all of the above. Maisy could have been a doggy decorator, with all marks she left throughout the walls and doors of our home. These were nothing in comparison, though, to the marks she left on my heart.

Christmas always brings back one of my favorite memories of Maisy. In 2007, when Maisy was four years old, my son and daughter came home with wrapped Christmas gifts that they had bought from the Santa Shop at school. There were gifts for the whole family, including Maisy, which they placed under the tree. The next day, we noticed Maisy chewing contentedly on something. One glance under the tree made it clear that she had opened one of her gifts ahead of Christmas morning, while leaving the others intact. Every Christmas afterwards, Maisy's gifts were placed on the fireplace mantel away from her inquiring nose. We didn't want her to spoil what Santa Claus had brought.

Having Maisy around was like having a sweet shadow. Everywhere I went in the house, she was right behind. Sometimes, if she had been resting, she would lose track of me. I could hear her searching every room. If I was sleeping with the covers over my head, Maisy would jump up onto the bed and sniff to make sure it was me. She would then curl up in a ball right next to me, and her contentment would be expressed through adorable sighs and other sweet sounds.

Maisy and I had so many fun times together, many of which were outdoors. Having her in my life was the definition of unconditional love. We went on boat rides at the lake, car rides to the pet store, and on more walks than I can count. I walked Maisy in the neighborhood, on nature trails, and even let her run off leash in nearby parks. We played fetch with a ball slinger if the spirit moved us. Maisy would stand at the ready waiting for the ball to launch, and when it did, she ran as fast as she could. I can still see her smiling face bringing the ball back to me each time. I loved our experiences, along with the quiet times when I snuggled next to her and just gazed onto her beautiful face.

The years flew by, the seasons changed, the children grew older, and so did Maisy. She had experienced some health issues in her life, primarily allergies that began in June and lasted through December. The veterinarian believed she had been allergic to some type of airborne pollen. It would start on her paws and Maisy would lick them until they were red and dry. From her paws, she would move on to lick other areas of her body. The allergies also caused ear and eye infections. To add to her maladies, Maisy experienced stomach issues. She wouldn't eat if she was upset, her stomach gurgling loudly as a sign. I could have opened a dog pharmacy with all of the drugs she'd been prescribed!

During the last year of her life, Maisy was on medication to control her persistent stomach issues. She was eating well until February 2017, when her appetite diminished; sometimes she rejected food altogether. Thinking this was more tummy trouble, I increased her dosage; it didn't help. Over the next couple weeks, her symptoms increased. She wouldn't eat anything. I tried putting honey on her mouth, but it held no appeal. She lacked interest in her well-known favorites including hamburger and beef sticks. Nothing worked.

When all options had been exhausted, we returned to the veterinarian. My thought was that the prognosis would lead to a different medication. The vet examined Maisy and drew some blood. The tests were fairly conclusive: Many of Maisy's lymph nodes were enlarged. The blood work indicated she had

Lymphoma. My vet asked if I wanted the name of a specialist. Besides the shock and heartbreak, I knew that, at age thirteen, I didn't want to put Maisy through any undue poking, prodding or heavy medications with severe side effects. She was a very nervous dog and having her endure intense treatment to extend her life another six months wasn't something I wanted for her or honestly, for me. Selfishly, I also thought of the time and money.

The vet said we could immediately begin a high dose of steroids. The steroids would increase her appetite and reduce her inflammation. She told me that each case was different, but steroids could extend Maisy's life by weeks or months. Eventually the steroids would no longer work, and we would lose Maisy.

When I got home, I was inconsolable. Despite the flood of emotions, I decided it best to start the steroid treatment and Maisy's appetite returned. It was a wonderful sight to see. Unfortunately, the steroids caused her to have insatiable thirst. Maisy's water bowls always became bone dry and she had to be let out often. At thirteen, her hearing was going, and it was difficult for her to jump on and off beds and to climb stairs. We woke up every night to lift her on and off the bed, fill her water bowl, and let her out.

After a few weeks, I started to reduce the steroids hoping Maisy's excessive thirst would end. It did not. She stopped eating, at one point not consuming anything for two days. She also started spitting up and struggled to swallow her steroid pill. Maisy had difficulty walking and was lethargic. I didn't want to leave her alone for extended periods of time, which also made it difficult for me to go to work. I was concerned with her increased thirst, potential accidents in our home, and watching her become increasingly weak. As difficult as it was, it occurred to me more and more that the best thing might be to have a veterinarian come to the house to end her life peacefully.

When the vet arrived, Maisy greeted her at the door. It was heartbreaking, but I think she knew. She hid in a corner under the desk. The vet was able to retrieve her and gradually administer the sedative. Maisy laid down and became very quiet. When the vet applied the second medication into her vein, the one that would end her life, she yelped. That broke my heart. As the medication flowed into her, I stayed by her side and stroked her continuously. During these final moments, I wanted her to hear my voice. I told her that I would always love her, that she was the best dog ever and that I was proud of her. Silently, she took her last breath. The date was March 14, 2017. Maisy was thirteen years and three months.

I knew that losing Maisy would be hard, but I wasn't prepared for what came next. I felt tremendous guilt and needed help. Why didn't I do more for her? Did I do it too soon? Why did I feel a sense of relief? I felt so selfish for being tired of trying to find something she would eat, like the chicken I boiled, the hamburger I cooked, the baby food I offered her. I had become tired of forcing medications down her throat and tired of being woken up in the middle of the night. No one else in my family seemed to feel the same level of grief or guilt. I reached out to the internet for help and found Beyond the Paw Print. I knew I needed to go to this support group.

When I attended my first meeting, I was a little nervous. I came armed with my pictures of Maisy, my grief, and my guilt. Some of the attendees seemed to know each other, and Micky, who facilitates the group, was warm and friendly. As the meeting went on, I started to feel more at ease. Listening to the many stories of love and loss made me realize that I wasn't in this alone. Micky then asked if I was comfortable enough to share my story. Difficult as it was, I did. Tears rolled down my cheeks as I went through the story of my Maisy, my life with her, my love for her and all that had happened at the end. Micky offered words of consolation and a good dose of professional wisdom, as well as resources and books. Micky also confirmed something I'd been thinking; that losing a pet can sometimes be as difficult as losing a person. A pet is always there for us, unconditionally, and their loss is almost more bittersweet than that of any human loss. I felt reassured that saying goodbye at home was a good decision, and that being able to hold and reassure her during those final moments was my final act of love.

After the meeting, I could feel some of the weight I carried being lifted off my shoulders. Additionally, when I spoke to people informally on our way out to the parking area, I felt comforted when a woman said every decision made for Maisy came completely out of love. It made me think I was being too hard on myself. Beyond the Paw Print offered healing through the support of others who have experienced the same grief. Even if I couldn't come to every meeting, I wanted to remain connected to the group to continue my healing process.

When I found BTPP, I found a safe place to express, understand and work my way through the grieving process. Writing Maisy's story for this book is my tribute to her and is part of my healing process. Even though she's no longer physically by my side, Maisy lives on in my memories and the words I have written about her for this story.

In reflection, I accept the decisions I made, and over time, both my grief and guilt have softened. I now think of all the wonderful memories and the good life Maisy and I had together. She will always be in my heart. Someday I'll be ready to bring another furry member into my family. For now, I'll continue to rely on BTPP and to encourage others who might be grieving the loss of a pet to attend one of their meetings, so they know they're not alone. Through the support of BTPP, I have been able to fill the void and ache in my heart with warm, loving memories, acceptance, and peace.

CERVANTES

STORY SIX

Bershert (Soulmate)

By Laura

It was May 1997, and the Detroit Zoo was holding its bi-annual pet adoption event. On a lark, my wife, Cathy and I decided to attend and check out the kittens. We hoped to adopt two, so they could be playmates and keep each other company.

We arrived during the event's final hours and most of the more desirable cats — i.e., the beautiful ones — had already been adopted, but I was fine with that. I looked at the rest, a kaleidoscope of unique features and personalities. Each kitty greeted me with meows and purrs, all competing for my attention. They were each adorable in their own way, but none was quite the one for me. As I made my way through the aisle of cages, I felt compelled to stop. Inside the cage directly in front of me, all alone, was an eight-week old kitty, a grey and white tabby. I was smitten.

He seemed shy, which made him even more appealing to me. I asked one of the volunteers to take him out so that I could hold him to get a better look. Never have I had a first encounter with a kitty like this — especially one who planted kisses all over my face. I knew from that moment forward I was his and he was mine. I called out to Cathy who was a couple tables over and also looking at kittens. She glanced at me and saw the kitten licking my face. "Is he the one?" she asked. All I could do was smile and nod.

I love unusual names for felines, so I named him Cervantes, after the Spanish author of the classic book, *Don Quixote*. I also often referred to him as My Little Man. We developed a strong bond as the years passed and I came to look upon him as my baby. His world seemed to center around me, and I loved that. Often, out of the corner of my eye, I would notice Cervantes staring at me as if I were the most wonderful thing in his world. This made me feel so special, knowing that he loved me above all. For the very first time, I felt loved unconditionally, without judgment.

I've always been close to my family, but there's something different when it comes to a human/animal relationship. It's simple and uncomplicated. My mother and Cathy would often comment that Cervantes was devoted to me first and foremost. Cathy would often say jokingly that she was the mother when I wasn't home, but when I walked through the door, I became the sole focus of Cervantes' attention. Anyone other than me was nice, but a lukewarm substitute.

I was always struck by how Cervantes was attuned to my daily habits. At the end of each workday, I'd find him waiting at the door for me. Our greeting went like this: I'd lean down to pick him up as he simultaneously lifted himself onto his hind legs and reached for me with his front paws. Incredible! No other cat has ever done this, before or after Cervantes. My boy also always knew when it was time to go to sleep. He would lay at the foot of the bed waiting for me to complete my nighttime routine. When I got in, he'd move onto my pillow, always sleeping with his back to me, which allowed me to fall asleep to the rhythm of his breathing and the sweet scent of his fur.

One night I had a most unusual dream about Cervantes. I dreamt he actually spoke to me, not in a human voice, but in a sort of toothy lisp emitting from his front teeth. The dream was so realistic that whenever I looked at him, I expected him to speak.

I would often say to him, "I know you can speak My Little Man. What is it you want to tell me?" It's illogical, I know, but I adored my Cervantes and so wanted him to tell me his every thought.

In early 2009, I noticed a significant change in my boy: His appetite had diminished and as a result, he began to lose weight. In the early phases of his illness, there were frequent visits to the veterinarian's office to discover the cause of these changes. I can still recall an incident that occurred at one of our appointments. I was in the waiting room with Cervantes sitting calmly on my lap. A few minutes later, another pet owner came through the door and noticed Cervantes as she approached the reception desk. I heard her whisper, "poor thing." I became very distressed because she voiced my greatest fear, that Cervantes was seriously ill. I wanted to yell out, "How dare you say that! My beloved, wonderful cat is NOT going to die!" In retrospect, I now understand that she didn't intend to upset me, but I would have felt less distressed if she had said something like, "Oh what a pretty kitty!"

Tests conducted by our veterinarian revealed that Cervantes had developed an over-active thyroid. Although there are different protocols, our vet recommended a series of radiation treatments, which Cervantes received throughout the summer. He was also placed on a special high-caloric food to boost his nutrition. Unfortunately, he continued to be lethargic and to lose weight. Despite all attempts to get the disease under control, his health didn't improve.

A few months later, on Election Day in November 2009, I went out to run an errand and received a call from Cathy telling me to come back immediately. I didn't have to ask why. I knew it was bad. When I got there, I paused and took a deep breath before opening the front door. Cathy was sitting on the couch next to our daughter Jessica, who was crying. Cathy took one look at me and simply shook her head. I knew he was gone. I went into the sun room where I found my boy motionless on the sofa as if he were asleep. This wonderful, beloved, twelve-year old creature who had been with me since he was eight weeks old, was gone. I had lost the one living breathing being that had loved me without condition, every single day of our lives together.

During the months after Cervantes' passing, I felt completely abandoned. Although I didn't really believe in it, I made an appointment with an animal communicator — a psychic — to see if Cervantes was trying to contact me. I was desperate, and needed comfort, somehow, somewhere. Our meeting took place over the phone. The communicator had a photo of Cervantes and told me how much he missed and loved me. It was a very emotional conversation. When we ended the phone call, I felt lost and alone. She spoke in generalities, unable to reveal anything specific about our life together. I began to worry that he really wasn't at the Rainbow Bridge.

I've never been the type of person who believed in signs from the dead. However, I knew that if there was a way for Cervantes to contact me, he would. I concluded that the communicator was simply a kind person trying to provide comfort. Although it might seem foolish, I felt compelled to contact another animal communicator. This individual said all the right things, but ultimately didn't make me feel any connection with my boy. I eventually recognized that I needed a more traditional form of support.

As the days turned into weeks and then months, it was apparent that I couldn't speak to my friends and family about Cervantes' death. Loved ones are there for you when a human being dies, but I find it sad that they don't know what to do when your pet dies. Otherwise well-meaning friends and family had limited patience with my grief. They often made dismissive statements like, "It's only a pet!" and expected the grieving to stop after a few weeks. Some of my friends told me that they received an entire week off from work after the death of a human family member. If I requested time off from work after the death of my dear cat, I'd be perceived as dramatic, or even worse, strange.

I felt lost without Cervantes. I began to feel myself going down the rabbit hole, caring less and less about things that normally were important to me. I didn't know it at the time, but I was falling into a deep depression. Going out meant nothing; sleep was all I wanted to do. It was even an effort to brush my teeth. All I wanted was to be with My Little Man. The depth of my depression was so severe that I even contemplated ending my life, honestly believing that it was the only thing that would stop the pain. I read the Rainbow Bridge poem repeatedly and yearned for our reunion there. My family despaired. Work kept me going and served as a helpful distraction. I could be animated with my co-workers and clients but always felt I was playing a part for eight hours a day. Home was where I could take off my makeup, get into my pajamas, and be alone with my sadness. My wife was doing her best to listen and be supportive, but I knew deep down she felt helpless. Depression is like quicksand: You know you're sinking but you give in because it's easier to surrender when you don't have enough energy to pull yourself out.

I searched online and found the pet loss support group, Beyond the Paw Print. Initially, I was uncertain if attending would help me, but I decided to go, to learn and listen. Initially, I found myself struggling as I listened to some of the stories. For example, when someone would say their cat or dog of twenty years died, I was jealous. Although my feelings were understandable, my persistent anger was stronger than my sensitivity toward others. I would think, "I only had my cat for twelve years, you had yours for 20!" It wasn't fair, and I wanted to lash out. I finally decided to seek therapy at the suggestion of the support group facilitator, Micky Golden Moore. She recognized the depression and rage that was just beneath the surface and was concerned about my well-being. I began therapy and continued to attend the meetings.

Eventually, I began to feel more empathy than bitterness. After attending the meetings for several months, I discovered that listening to other like-minded people gave me the strength to heal. These meetings provided many insights for me. I learned that I wasn't alone, that my grief was legitimate, my feelings were real, and I was going to be okay. In time, I found myself giving advice to new attendees who were inconsolable after the recent passing of their animals. We all shared a common bond: a love for our animals.

About six months after the death of Cervantes, I attended yet another pet adoption event at our local zoo. I found a kitty who was the mirror image of Cervantes. When I was told that he was a real mama's boy, I decided to adopt little Cannoli on the spot! I knew it wasn't realistic, but I thought by adopting this look-alike, I could have my Cervantes back in some way, shape, or form. I soon discovered that this little guy had a personality all his own. Oddly, we were unable to bond at first, but Cathy showered him with affection. Eventually, he and I did come together, but it was almost four years before I was able to open my heart fully to love again.

As the years passed my despair did lift. I felt periods of sadness, but I also felt moments of great happiness when I looked at pictures of Cervantes. I started fostering cats for a local rescue, finding that I enjoyed being able to socialize them which in turn gave them a better chance of finding a forever home. It helped me to recognize that we all have room in our hearts to love again. I believe our deceased companions would want us to adopt another pet, to give them a loving nickname and a plush toy, just as they had received. I also believe that our deceased pets secretly appear like ghosts in the night and whisper sweet messages to our new companions like, "You hit the jackpot with this owner buddy!" I imagine them telling our new companion about the wonderful life that lies ahead and all the love they're going to receive.

So now I divide my life into two categories: pre-November 2009 and post-November 2009. Although it has been several years since Cervantes passed, the experience has taken quite a toll on me. His death has been the most devastating event I've ever experienced. Truth be told, I managed to get through the one other truly significant loss, the death of my father, much better than the death of my beloved cat. I have learned that others have had similar experiences; and this has helped me in my journey to reconcile these losses.

To honor the life of Cervantes, I had the imprint of his paw along with his name tattooed on my back with the Hebrew word *Beshert*, which means "soulmate." We were meant for each other, of that I'm sure. I keep Cervantes' ashes in a beautiful urn on a mantel beside my bed, so I see him every night. A few times a year, and on the anniversary of his death, I pick the urn up and while holding it, tell him how much I love him. Time does heal all wounds.

Now, when I look at pictures of My Little Man, I smile with gratitude that this angelic creature and I found each other. There are people out there who know *exactly* what you're going through and will gladly give you a hug when it feels like you're going to break. I am so thankful I found the BTPP Support Group to lean on and to help me through the most challenging period of my life. I made it when I didn't think I could. There's no magic pill to get you through this hard time, but being with those who care, those who "get it," really does help. You can make it, and yes, it does get better.

HERSHEY

STORY SEVEN

The Hershey Legend

By Ric and Paula

When Paula and I first met Hershey, he was six months old and belonged to the friend of a friend. His name at that time was Dave. His owners had subsequently needed a sitter for him while they were away on vacation, and our friend told them about us. We were all too happy to step in to look after their little guy. Those few days with Dave turned out to be pure joy. What a sweet boy he was! It was then that we realized we wanted a Dachshund.

In the midst of our search, Dave's owners had been searching for answers of their own. They were concerned that their other dog, a Great Dane, might unintentionally step on little Dave, causing injury. The owners saw how much we cared for their dog, and, most unexpectedly and happily, offered him to us. We were delighted!

Our first priority, though, was to change his name. We really didn't like it, so we started to think of other possibilities. One day, Dave was snooping around in Paula's purse. When we looked to see what was capturing his attention, we realized it was Paula's Hershey bar. That's when we decided that Dave would be known as Hershey. With that, the legend began.

Hershey became Paula's constant companion, never far from mom and her lap; always ready to give out a nose lick, which we aptly called "Hershey Kisses." He loved to lounge on our deck and smell all the flowers we had planted there. When he was really relaxed, he would go into a full recline position to soak up the sunshine. Hershey was our first little dog; and was the greatest friend anyone could hope for. Anytime there was a picture being taken, he was right there, front and center. It was six years of happy times for all of us. Then abruptly and without warning, it all went bad, so very bad.

When we saw that Hershey wasn't acting like himself, we took him immediately to the vet. We were willing to do anything and everything that might make Hershey feel better. Paula took Hershey to the vet's office every morning on her way to work since no one was at home to watch him during the day. He was given daily fluid injections to sustain his hydration. Devoted mom that she was, Paula would pick Hershey up after work every night, his IV still attached, providing the necessary hydration that would sustain him overnight.

This protocol continued for a week, but then Hershey needed to have surgery—and quickly, when we learned he had suffered a ruptured anal gland. It went well, but he needed to remain at the veterinary hospital for a week to recover. This was a horrible time for us. We hated that he could not be at home and visited him every night. The drive there was fine, because we knew we would see our boy; the ride home though was horrible. Seeing the look in his eyes, when we had to leave was heartbreaking. You could see the confusion, his wondering what was wrong, almost as if he were thinking, "Did I do something wrong? Why are you not taking me home?" We felt utterly helpless, unable to make him understand why we couldn't stay, or why he couldn't come home.

Then, finally, we were given a discharge date! As the day approached, we were so much more than excited—we could not *wait*! At 6:00 a.m. that morning the phone rang and Paula picked it up only to hear the vet on the other end of the line. He told her that Hershey had had trouble breathing and despite his best efforts, they couldn't save him.

To say we were devastated does not even begin to describe the pain. Our lives changed on March 23, 2012, when Hershey, the world's greatest mini-wiener dog, passed over the Rainbow Bridge. Our little man was no longer ours. We existed in a state of anguish and despair. Living ceased for us. Activities beyond work were forgotten. People were an annoyance. Two of our five children still lived at home, but the atmosphere was devoid of joy. Life as we knew it had changed. The kids knew how much we loved our boy, but they were unable to console or help us return to normal. Our normal was gone.

Months passed with no change. The black spiral of depression had us in its eye, a perfect storm of grief. I hated the life we were leading, so I searched the internet for help. Something had to change. I came across Beyond the Paw Print, a pet loss support group, and I knew we had to go.

After almost a full year of grieving, we attended our first meeting. *It was terrible*. Hearing others talk about their losses was hard enough, but to tell our story was even harder! The wound reopened; we were overwhelmed with pain as the tears cascaded. How can this possibly be a positive thing? Yet we returned to the meetings, again and again, hoping that at some point the pain would begin to ease. With time it did, and as with a wound, it heals again each time it reopens. Unfortunately, the pain never disappears; it becomes a scar that marks your heart, mind, and soul. We all live with these emotional scars, do we not?

After attending a few BTPP meetings, something unexpected began to happen. We started to look forward to them. We came to realize that going to the meetings helped heal our wounds, and that we weren't alone. There were others who felt the same way we did about our animals. They are not just pets, they are family.

As time passed, we discovered that we had the ability to support new group members, while requiring less consolation for ourselves. The group dynamic at BTPP shifts, but never deviates from a course of support and compassion to all in need. Micky Golden Moore is an earthbound angel. How else can her work be explained? There is no monetary gain, no fame. Husband Bud Moore is also behind the curtain, supporting his partner always, yet staying hidden. What an awesome pair they make. With nowhere to turn, and no one who understood the depth of our pain, we learned that help is available and waiting, through Micky and the amazing people who attend the BTPP meetings. It is not an easy task, to share your grief and participate in these sessions, but it will change you. We have come to learn that there is no progress without pain.

Our loss has altered us in profound ways. We have become better people, with a heightened sense of improving our planet, and more empathy toward all who suffer. For us, these were the desirable side effects of BTPP meetings. We continue to rescue animals in need. This is a lifestyle, not a hobby. All creatures deserve safe haven, good food, and someone to care for them.

One day, while searching the internet, a story about a police dog who was being retired caught my eye. I read the story and looked at the photos, which showed the dog in a wheelchair. And then something extraordinary happened: Hershey had never spoken to me in life, but he did then. Clear as a bell, I heard him say, "Dad, you can make those. You can make anything!" So I did.

WEE WEELZ became a reality. The name represents what I create: wheels and wheelchairs made for an animal's mobility, all free of charge. As I am a lifelong machinist and mechanic with a full shop at my disposal, I can construct just about anything. I'm not a huge self-promoter although I have put my cards on a few well-known sites, under the board, "The Roll It Forward Pet Mobility Project." My biggest fear is that I'll be inundated with requests, so I intentionally retain a low profile to avoid delay in the delivery of my WEE WEELZ product.

Although most of the animals I help are small, I design and build wheelchairs for any furry friend, any condition, anywhere worldwide; no one is refused. My specialty is known as a "quad cart," made for animal friends who have the need or desire to go strolling but lack the ability to walk. They're like a mini shopping cart used for steering. I've made quad carts for rabbits, and several small and medium-sized dogs. WEE WEELZ units have been delivered throughout the United States, as well as to Africa, Egypt, England, and Ireland. It feeds my soul to help our furry friends live longer and in greater comfort with loved ones.

Hershey was sent to us as a teacher, I can see that now. He taught us how to cope with loss, how to grieve, and how to move forward – at such a cost, yes, but the lessons remain. Since then, we have endured additional human and pet losses; of them all, Hershey's lessons have been the most valuable. Thank you, my furry son.

JAKE

STORY EIGHT

My Protector

By Sue

"Can I pleeeeeeeeeeeeeeeease get a puppy?" It was a question I had asked my parents repeatedly growing up. The answer was always the same: "When you have a place to keep it, we will get you a puppy."

Apparently, my bedroom wasn't the kind of place they had in mind. Given the circumstances, and since I'd wanted a dog for as long as I could remember, getting a home of my own couldn't happen fast enough. Just thinking about having a puppy melted my heart. I decided it would be a Golden Retriever. Who could resist their cute little faces?

As a grown woman with a full-time job, I finally purchased a condominium and began prepping it for my future canine companion. I built a deck off the back, almost solely for the prevention of muddy paws on my new carpet. I was ready! I just had to decide if a puppy truly fit the lifestyle of a single girl. Working full time kept me busy, and I reconsidered the needs and responsibility that would come with adopting a younger dog. With that, I decided that adopting a more mature dog would be a better idea. After all, they needed a home and love too.

I started my search and online adoption sites became my

first stop. I made a list of the local rescue shelters, calling each one to ask if they currently had any Golden Retrievers. Since the breed is so docile — and popular — 99 percent of the shelters said no. There was one, though, that didn't. "Are you missing your dog?" the woman on the other end of the phone asked me. I said no; but was looking to adopt. She informed me that a Golden Retriever had just come in that day, but that they were pretty sure they had seen him before and that he'd be claimed. If I were interested though, I could come down to meet him. I quickly jumped in my car and drove to the shelter. Had I known what was about to happen, I would have tried to prepare my heart.

I walked in and the woman at the front desk took me to the back. Every dog in the place started barking the minute she opened the door, as if to say, "Hello! Come see me! Look at me!" The sounds were pure joy to my heart. As soon as we got to the kennel of the resident Retriever, he stopped barking, sat down nicely and let me pet him. His name was a mystery, since he had no tags hanging from his collar. The shelter assistant took him out of his kennel and let us spend time together in the "Family Room," just the two of us.

I introduced myself, told the sweet dog how sorry I was that he had gotten lost, and that if his family didn't pick him up during the three-day holding period, I would take him home with me. We played catch, I scratched his ears, rubbed his belly, and of course, gave him some treats. Heaven on earth. The hardest part was saying goodbye – and waiting to see if he'd be claimed. I had already decided I was going to name him Jake. The volunteers at the shelter started calling him by his new name right away.

I called the shelter at least twice a day to see if Jake was still there and went to see him every day after work. Finally, the blessed moment arrived: Jake's holding period was up and he could be adopted! I called first thing in the morning and they confirmed that he was still at the shelter. I drove over with a new leash, collar and ID tag. In a very short time, Jake would officially belong to me. I would do everything in my power to prevent him from ever getting lost again. I was excited, but nervous, and most of all very, very happy.

From the minute I brought Jake home, he settled right in. We figured out how best to communicate with each other and quickly fell into a routine. Jake loved to go for walks and car rides, and was a huge snuggle bunny. He loved people, but he was not all that fond of other dogs. Perhaps his short stay at the shelter had something to do with that. Jake was ever the gentleman and the only time he would bark was if he could see me but not get to me. He always needed to be by my side. He was my protector.

On our first visit to the vet, I learned that Jake was about four years old. Since he was a stray, he had arrived at the shelter without any paperwork, so his age was a guess. My solution: We would share birthdays, since I had adopted him pretty close to my own. It quickly became my favorite day on the calendar.

With condo living — i.e. no backyard — Jake always had to be on a leash. We would venture to parks where he could run but giving him his own yard was something I really wanted. A few years later, I sold the condominium and we moved into a house. I had found the perfect place, complete with the yard we'd always wanted.

The first time I brought him to our new home, Jake didn't want to get out of the car. I encouraged him and reminded him how much I loved him, and that wherever he was, I would be there too. When Jake finally felt safe, he jumped out of the car, sniffed around his new backyard and gave his approval with a wagging tail!

Jake was a healthy, happy puppy who brightened the lives of everyone in my family. We took long walks every day. Jake became my travel companion on family trips to northern Michigan. We explored new areas and met lots of new friends along the way. Golden Retrievers are incredibly friendly and curious, and Jake enjoyed greeting everyone we came into contact with on our daily sojourns.

Just before his twelfth birthday, our lives were forever changed. We went in for Jake's annual check-up and an X-ray revealed that his liver was enlarged. The vet was concerned so he sent us for additional tests. Those results came back inconclusive, but the possibility of pre-cancerous cells was mentioned. We were advised to keep an eye on his condition, so I made plans to follow up with our regular vet in a few weeks.

Everything about Jake continued to be normal. He was eating as he always did, acting the same, and continuing to do all the things he loved. Just two short weeks later though, my life turned upside down. My nephew and I attended a hockey game and had gotten home late. I had let Jake outside when we arrived and proceeded to settle my nephew in for the night. Then, after getting myself ready for bed, I thought it would be a good idea to let Jake out once more. When he came in, he started licking his leg. When I looked to see what it was, I saw blood. What was in my very dog-safe yard that could have caused this? It was then that I noticed that it wasn't his leg: Jake was bleeding from his nose. I tried not to worry but to instead be proactive, and quickly called the after-hours emergency vet. They instructed me to put a cold compress on it and call back if the bleeding didn't stop. The compress reduced the bleeding, but then Jake sneezed, and it started all over again. Panic set in.

I called my parents, who raced over, my mom staying with my sleeping nephew while my dad and I took Jake to the ER. The vet quickly sedated him and was able to get the bleeding and sneezing to stop. They wanted to keep Jake overnight for observation. It tore my heart in two having to leave him like that. Happily, the vet called a few hours later to let us know that the bleeding had stopped, Jake was finally resting, and I could probably take him home the next day. I stayed awake the entire night.

After that came a series of events that are still painful to recall. Several days later Jake was diagnosed with lymphoma. Under the advice of our vet, he began treatment at an animal hospital that specialized in cancer care. The diagnosis was very hard to accept and even harder to comprehend, despite the animal hospital staff being kind and compassionate. They gave me time to cry, as well as the time and space to just be with Jake. I couldn't have asked for anything better for either of us during such a difficult time.

The veterinarians wanted to keep a close eye on Jake after his new diagnosis, so I had to leave him overnight. It was so hard to do this, but they were nice enough to take my phone calls at all hours and to provide updates. Once the vets stabilized Jake, they put a treatment plan in place, and I could then visit him during his stay. Two days later, I brought him home. The plan included treatments at the vet's office once a week, but at least he could remain at home with me, and rest. One week into his treatments, I recognized that Jake was in serious pain and suffering. My love for him was so deep, I didn't want to lose him, but I certainly didn't want him to suffer. He had been so good to me, I needed to be good to him.

After a couple of not-so-great-days, and a really bad night, I knew in my heart that it was time to say goodbye. How could I let him suffer when he had been so loyal, so loving? I called my parents and told them of my decision. I asked if they could accompany us to the vet. My dad was out of town, but my mom arrived within minutes. I also called my brother Mike, and he came over too.

Jake was too weak to walk, so my brother carried him to the car. As I sat in the back seat with him giving him his favorite treat — cheese — I told Jake how proud I was of him and how brave he had been. I thanked him for being my best friend and for always protecting and loving me. I wanted the car ride to last forever, but we arrived at the vet all too quickly. My brother carried him inside and we were immediately escorted into a room.

Our regular vet was out of town this particular day, however, his wife – also a vet, and a friend of mine from high school – was there. God certainly had orchestrated this. Friends of mine, who happened to be coming in from out of town for other reasons and had been checking in on Jake regularly, raced there to be with me. I had later found out these friends drove close to 100 mph to be there. I am so blessed to have so many wonderful people in my life!

There were so many of us there that we had to move to a bigger room, one usually reserved for surgery. I will always be grateful that Jake and I were surrounded by our family and close friends and the wonderful, amazing veterinary staff that loved and took care of us for so many years. They gave me as much time as I needed to say goodbye. It was so hard, and so tearful, and to this day is still very emotional to recall. Just as we were saying goodbye, my mom's phone rang. It was my dad. He somehow knew to call right at that exact moment so he could say goodbye too. In just two short weeks from when it all started, I bid farewell to my very best friend. My heart would never be the same.

The drive home and the next several days were a blur. My sister Heather, who wasn't able to be with me at the vet, met us at home to offer love and support. She called me every day and came over many times to be with me. Family and friends checked in to see how I was doing. I received flowers and beautiful gifts with Jake's picture from friends far away. It was so touching.

Despite all the love and support I received, from the cancer clinic where they lovingly cared for Jake, as well as our vet, I struggled through the next several weeks like I've never struggled before. I didn't remember what day it was. I would get to work and realize I had forgotten my laptop at home. I missed appointments. Life was a blur. I didn't want to be at home, but then when I wasn't at home, I would panic wondering who was going to let Jake out? Who was going to feed him? I didn't know how to process my grief. I started searching online for pet loss support groups and found Beyond the Paw Print. I immediately emailed Dr. Micky Golden Moore. I couldn't believe how quickly she replied! Perhaps this will work, I thought. Perhaps there is someone else out there who understands this deep pain I'm in and can help.

I attended a meeting and was so thankful for the time Micky gave me to tell my story, to cry, and to grieve. I was very glad to be with others who understood this type of pain, a pain that only others who have had to say goodbye to a furry baby can understand. Micky provided resources, handouts, and books, as well as her time and love to help those of us who were where she had once been. I attended the monthly support group meetings for about five months, until I was able to accept that Jake had crossed the Rainbow Bridge, and that I had done everything I could to love and care for him. I know someday we will be reunited.

One of my treasured memories of this time period, was when I had the opportunity to attend a BTPP remembrance service, led by Micky. We don't often think about having a service like this for our animal companions, but they are family. Some people may laugh at the thought of this, but it's true. The bond we share with our animal companions is pure unconditional love. Who wouldn't grieve after seeing them for the last time? I attended the remembrance service with others from our group and we celebrated the beautiful lives we had shared with our companions, the lives that had brought us so much happiness, laughter, and joy. I realized that their lives had made ours fuller and so much more complete. I will forever be thankful for that beautiful day.

It's been nine years since I had to say goodbye to Jake. I miss him every day, but I know he's with me, and still protecting me. About six months after he died, in a series of events that I'm sure Jakey had a paw in, a new Golden Retriever wiggled his way into my heart. I knew he was picked by Jake himself, since my new friend's name was also Jake. We soon changed it to Joey and welcomed him into our home.

To those who are grieving, my heart goes out to you. I understand the deep pain and the hole that's left in your heart. Give yourself time. Do something that honors your companion. Jake loved ice cream, so after his passing I sent our vet ice cream gift cards in honor of our beloved dog. Write your baby a letter. Tell them how much you miss them and how much they brought to your life. Buy a charm of a dog or cat, or the initial of their name and wear it on a necklace. Make a memory box. I put all of Jake's pictures on a flash drive and downloaded them onto an electronic frame so they would play on a continuous loop. The visual display is a comfort for me and an easy way to see him at any given time.

Above all, be patient with yourself during a difficult time. Our animals are a big part of our lives and it will take time to get used to them not being there. When Jake passed, a friend sent me a memorial stone that to this day rings true in my heart: "If love could have saved you, you would have lived forever."

SAPPHIRE

STORY NINE

Sea Glass Love

By Carol and Jim

WE MET OUR KITTY IN A MOST AGREEABLE WAY. My husband is an avid gardener and has spent his summers doing what he enjoys most: working in the yard. One afternoon, a darling little cat strolled into our midst, demanding our attention with loud meows and other delightful sounds. The cat returned for a visit just about every day that summer.

As temperatures started to cool, we became concerned for our little friend's well-being. One day, while in the kitchen, I looked up and there she was, sitting on my windowsill, looking straight at me. I knew she needed to be taken in. When I approached her, the kitty proved very sweet and allowed me to pick her up immediately. That was all I needed. She was meant for us.

When it came time to give this beautiful feline a name, my husband thought back to a television show he had watched as a child and to one of the characters named Sapphire. He had always liked the name, and it seemed to fit her sparkling personality. With Sapphire laying calmly in my arms, our first stop was to the groomer, and then to the veterinarian for a full check-up. Our vet estimated that Sapphire was about six months old, but also made an unwelcome discovery. He found an abscess in her neck, that resulted in a serious blood infection. Sapphire underwent surgery, was placed on antibiotics and remained at the hospital for about four days. Fortunately, her ailments were treatable, and we were happy to nurse her back to health.

What we learned most about our new kitty was the extent of her intelligence. Sapphire had chosen us. Somehow, she trusted that we would love and care for her and make her health and well-being a priority. Without us, her life would have been snuffed out by the maladies that had plagued her, which proved easily manageable with medical attention. As pet owners quite often say, she saved us as much as we saved her.

Sapphire was a gem (pun intended!). At the time we took her in, I was working in a demanding job and sometimes came home tired and frustrated. I could always count on my girl running to the door to greet me. All the tribulations of the day vanished immediately. The unconditional love she provided was the one constant in our lives. Sapphire could even discern those times we needed extra attention. When I lost my Mom, she helped to heal my broken heart. Friends may have grown weary of my mourning, but Sapphire was always by my side or on my lap, ready to provide comfort and a cuddle.

Uncharacteristically for a cat, Sapphire loved to ride in the car and often accompanied me on my errands around town. That's right! She always behaved, sitting up tall in her pretty basket. When other drivers saw a cat sitting in the passenger seat, they would smile or wave with delight. What a wonderful companion!

The years passed and we were very fortunate that Sapphire stayed in excellent health for so long. All that changed in her fourteenth year. I was out of town visiting family when my husband called and said he was concerned about our girl. Jim noticed that her appetite had diminished, and she seemed to have an increased thirst as well. Of course, I flew home right away, and we went to our veterinarian as soon as possible. He delivered the bad news that Sapphire was in the initial stages of irreversible kidney failure. With our vet's exceptional knowledge and loving care, we were able to sustain her life for four more wonderful years through fluid injections under the skin. These treatments provided the hydration she needed to survive and thrive. We felt we had been given a gift and treasured every single day we had with our precious cat.

Midway through the eighteenth year of Sapphire's life, our local church hosted a Blessing of the Animals service, the timing for which couldn't have been better. Sapphire's health was in decline and I believed this service would bring comfort to both of us. We took our place in the pew and Sapphire sat quietly next to me, not in a carrier or on a leash. She never attempted to jump out, nor did she react to the many dogs that were running up and down the aisle. The pastor was very kind and appeared to be a true animal lover. He sat down next to us at one point and said a prayer and a blessing for Sapphire. It was an amazing experience, filled with laughter as well as tears. I had always wanted to attend this service and am so grateful that Sapphire was able to receive this special blessing before her death, only two short weeks later.

My girl had always been very active and affectionate. In the days before we lost her, she became very lethargic and slept much more than usual. She had also started to have "accidents" that were very much out of character. One evening, she lay on the bed next to me and didn't move the entire night. When I awoke, I saw that she'd had an accident. I picked her up and the look on her face said it all. After four years of treatment, at age eighteen, my girl was ready to say goodbye.

We called the vet and took Sapphire to his office immediately. She was given an injection and died peacefully. We stayed in the room with her for about a half hour, but then had to return home to our empty house. It was one of the most difficult days of our lives, but we knew that we had done for her what she had always done for us, and that was to provide unconditional love. We were blessed to be able to give back that love when she needed it the most, to put Sapphire's needs ahead of our own. After we left, neither my husband nor I could catch our breath. The loss of our sweet cat was beyond heartbreaking.

After Sapphire received her angel wings, I was numb with grief. I sought comfort from my friends, but we all grieve differently and not everyone understands the whirlwind of emotions associated with the loss of a beloved animal. It was our veterinarian's office who recommended that we reach out to Beyond the Paw Print and its founder, Dr. Micky Golden Moore.

After talking to Micky, I knew immediately that I was going to be OK. Our phone conversation provided the support and understanding I needed. With the meeting almost a month away, Micky invited me to meet at a local café where I was able to share my story and my grief. The following month, I attended the BTPP meeting where I found the support I sought. Through the group, I learned that so many others experienced a sense of loss similar to my own. Friendships were formed and the healing began.

As time passed, I realized that I wanted to do something special in Sapphire's memory. I wrote thank you notes to the friends who had sent messages of condolence and flowers to our home; we weren't the only ones who thought she was such a special girl.

But apart from that, I knew I had to stay busy and was determined to find a way to keep a part of Sapphire with me. Despite having no experience, I designed a bracelet with a charm containing one of my favorite pictures of Sapphire. I wore that bracelet every day, for a very long time, and still occasionally wear it now, finding great comfort in having her picture on my wrist. I also made a key chain with a picture of the two of us in the car and keep it in the vehicle, so Sapphire could continue to travel alongside us. I spread some of her ashes under her favorite tree where she spent many wonderful summer days lying in the warm sun, and I planted a garden in that spot as well. Each summer when I look out the kitchen window, I see the flowers and know Sapphire is there with us, shining bright.

One of my favorite hobbies growing up on the east coast of Maryland was collecting sea glass. I keep a collection of it in my home office. Through many years of gathering the glass from various beaches, I've discovered that it comes in many different shapes and sizes. Amazingly, I was able to find four oddly shaped pieces that, when put together, spelled out the word "Love." Was this a coincidence? Perhaps, but nothing like this has ever happened before or after any of my sea glass searches. These four pieces and Sapphire's ashes sit together on a shelf, a treasure trove of objects that remind us of our beautiful girl.

Two years after Sapphire passed away, I received an invitation from Micky to attend the BTPP memorial service she was leading. The ceremony provided closure that had very much eluded me and was also an opportunity to publicly acknowledge and honor Sapphire. How wonderful to gather together with so many others who understood the terrible loss I felt. We talked, laughed, cried, and shared our stories. Even through the tears, I found the sadness had lessened and felt at peace, maybe for the very first time since Sapphire's passing.

Now that we're retirees, we are on the go quite a bit and haven't adopted a new kitty. Instead, we get comfort from feeding the feral cats who visit our property and we check on their well-being as best we can from a gentle distance. We also support two local shelters in Sapphire's memory.

Our girl has been gone for almost four years, and we both miss her every day. How blessed we were to have had Sapphire with us for eighteen and a half incredible years and that this beautiful little girl strolled into our yard on that blissful summer day. It's amazing what an impact a seven-pound bundle of fur had on our lives. Even now, I tear up thinking about sweet Sapphire. We have so many happy memories and treasure all of them. At Christmastime, we even bought Sapphire her own little tree and spoiled her with special kitty gifts. I still put that tree up every year and hang the needlepoint stocking ornament I made for her front and center.

I once read an online post that said, "Do not cry because it is over, but smile because it was." On the days when I still miss my Sapphire, I try to smile and remember how grateful we are to have had her. There will always be only one Sapphire, of that we can be sure.

KNUCKLES

STORY TEN

My Guardian Angel

By Lindsay

I WAS IDLY FLIPPING THROUGH the television channels one night when I came upon a news segment on dogs up for adoption at our local Humane Society. An eight-month-old pooch named Woody was being featured, a brindle Boxer and American Pit Bull Terrier mix, and I was immediately smitten. He had large, soulful eyes and ears that protruded sideways from his giant head. I'm not sure if the shelter staff named him Woody because he was a stray discovered on Woodmen Road, or because his striking dark brindle coat was reminiscent of rich wood paneling.

My husband and I went to the shelter a few days later to meet him. Never had I been met with such enthusiasm! Never in my life had I seen a creature, of any species, so excited to be in my presence! The deal was sealed, and an hour later, Woody came home with us. It soon hit me though that I had taken on something huge. This was the first dog I had as an adult. It wasn't my parent's dog – it was *my* dog. Suddenly, we found ourselves responsible for the well-being of someone who totally relied on us.

We also recognized that Woody would require a significant amount of our time for training, feeding, attention, and care. What I had yet to discover was the true magnitude of love I would receive from him. Woody was about to join me, an adult woman, on a decade-long roller coaster ride, demonstrating his unconditional love, forgiveness, presence, and unwavering protection.

Woody's animated personality reminded me of the Sega Genesis video game console character Sonic the Hedgehog, and especially of Sonic's friend and rival, Knuckles. The latter had incredible stamina, could run and play for hours on end, was physically strong, and had some hilarious jumps and spins due to his martial arts skills. The name Knuckles just fit my dog.

As the wife of an active duty service member, I spent time with everyone but my spouse. We were married during Operation Iraqi Freedom and Operation Enduring Freedom, and my husband was often gone from home, either in training or deployed. During the difficult and lonely times, Knuckles became my confidant and my motivation to get out of bed in the morning, to keep going and face the day. I quickly recognized how my dog depended on me *and* how much I depended on him. On my own and far away from my family, in an increasingly unhealthy marriage, Knuckles was the one bright spot in my life. He kept me busy and distracted.

We were stationed in Colorado, lucky enough to live along the beautiful front of the Cheyenne Mountain range. Knuckles and I spent most days hiking for hours on the breathtaking trails. To say my dog was high-energy is an understatement! While I was at work, Knuckles spent eight to twelve hours at doggy daycare, running around, burning off his nonstop energy.

On my days off, we visited the nearby dog park so he could play with his other brindle Boxer friend, Zeke. On other days, we'd visit the neighborhood high school where we'd play on the baseball field. Knuckles *loved* playing ball! I'd whip a tennis ball across the field and when he returned it to me, we'd trade it for another one. He'd drop his while I presented a new tennis ball. Knuckles was very intelligent. It didn't take long for him to learn that when I didn't return the ball it meant we were done playing and about to head home. I'd always let him proudly carry the ball in his mouth on the walk back. Knuckles was also quite the soccer player: He excelled at defense and made several hilariously memorable saves when acting as goalie.

Not only did Knuckles have boundless physical energy, he possessed a natural curiosity. He was a dog who needed a "job," otherwise he'd entertain himself with the kind of activity that was fun for him, but not for me, like destroying a down feather pillow while running around the house. On another occasion, he ripped the mini-blinds off the window so he could better observe the activities of the outside world. I never gave my parents enough credit for raising our family dogs! This was a huge learning experience.

I will admit that I had no idea what I was doing and realized the only thing I *could* do was enlist the help of a dog trainer. I decided if we were going to be in this for the long haul, we had to be on the same page. Our trainer was fantastic. His primary line of work was training military working dogs. Prior to his moving to Colorado, he was in charge of the Boston Police Department's K9 unit. Knuckles flourished under his tutelage and revealed his high level of intelligence. We went from basic obedience to advanced obedience to Canine Good Citizen certification in no time. The Canine Good Citizen certification program was five weeks long; five sessions at 60 minutes per session.

Next came the certification exam. Of course, Knuckles excelled and earned his new designation as a Canine Good Citizen, becoming an amazing ambassador for his breed. He was also happiest when challenged to work his mind along with his body. Not only did the training fulfill Knuckle's energy requirements, our relationship improved immensely. Our bond and mutual trust grew even stronger. After Knuckles completed all of his training, I continued privately with K9 protection training and was amazed at how this additional work enhanced his confidence. Since my husband was often away, Knuckles helped me feel protected and safe. Unexpectedly, I learned a lot about myself through this whole process, seeing how Knuckles responded to my positive or negative energy. I witnessed just how powerful the connection is between canines and humans.

During the course of my seven-year marriage, my husband and I moved across the country countless times since part of his military service involved taking on new deployments at various bases. When we were headed somewhere new, my cats, Knuckles, and even my birds, accompanied us. I've had parrots my entire life, four while I was married: a Quaker parrot, a Sulfur-Crested Cockatoo, a Fischer Lovebird, and a Patagonian Conure. We also had three cats: Mickey, Katie and Brow. There was no debate, they were part of the package. My animals were my family. Knuckles, moreover, was best friends with my Maine Coon cat, Mickey, whom I had adopted only a short time after Knuckles came into our lives. Wherever Knuckles went, Mickey went, and vice versa; they were each other's shadow. The two had become so accustomed to the military lifestyle of moving and road trips that they would sleep curled up together on Knuckles' dog bed in the back seat.

Call it naiveté, our life together was so blissful, it never occurred to me that we wouldn't be together forever. I knew one day Knuckles would get older and slow down, but I never expected that to actually happen, or for him to actually *leave*. Maybe I was avoiding the inevitable, which I tend to do. The problem was, Knuckles truly was my life. He had become my therapist, my partner, my child, my *everything*, especially during and after my divorce, when he was pretty much the only consistent part of my life. Knuckles didn't care how much money was in my bank account, or if my eyes were bloodshot from crying. He didn't care that my new midnight addiction to Cinnamon Toast Crunch had caused my pants to split. Knuckles was just happy to be with me. The life of a dog is so simple and pure: they don't live in the past and they don't care about the everyday drama. Knuckles kept me grounded in the present.

But the inevitable did happen: Knuckles developed end-stage osteoarthritis as well as an acute neurological condition, both of which were quickly diminishing his quality of life. I knew my dog, and he was miserable. No matter how many veterinarians we consulted to get a second, third, or fourth opinion, the fact was that he was *never* going to get better. Knuckles was now eleven and a half years old and his prognosis was poor. No amount of treatment or money would be able to make him well again. He no longer wanted to eat and despite my creativity in administering his medications, he refused all of it. He was unable to get up on his own, play with toys, or groom himself. Knuckles had completely pulled away, no longer wanting affection or enjoying life. He was in chronic pain. During his last days on this earth, Knuckles' feline friend, Mickey, was still by his side, curled up next to him like he'd always been. I believe Mickey knew his best friend was dying and chose to stay with him as long as he could, to provide him with the comfort he needed. I knew in my heart that my dog was ready to leave, but I wasn't ready to have that happen. We had spent over a decade together, but I still felt cheated and wanted more time. Eventually, I knew I had to let him go with some amount of dignity. He deserved that.

Given my fifteen years of experience as a certified nursing assistant in home health care, hospitals, long term care facilities, and hospice, I've seen my fair share of death. Survival in this field is quite simple: a certain level of desensitization is required, otherwise, you can't perform. Your patients rely on your strength. Due to my hospice background, I fully understand the physiology of dying, but experience and emotion aren't mutually exclusive. On December 1, 2017, at 4:40 p.m., no amount of training prepared me for the moment Knuckles died. When he slipped away, I felt the most intense pang of relief that he was no longer suffering. That moment was followed immediately by one of overwhelming sadness and crushing guilt. The depth of these feelings was unlike anything I've ever experienced. I felt dizzy, nauseous, and empty. When he left, part of me left with him. I buried my face in his warm, muscular chest and let out a gut-wrenching scream. He was gone and I had been the one to make that decision.

The only thing left behind were the massive medical bills I'd accumulated over the last couple weeks of his life. I had spent money I didn't have to ensure that Knuckles received the care he needed, from routine to emergency care. I had sacrificed my credit and taken out a personal loan to ensure he got the best that money could buy, regardless of the cost. Although I'll be paying it off for years to come, I wouldn't change a thing. Knuckles was worth every single penny.

We all face the same fate. However, I am haunted by the fact that I had to make that decision and choose this fate for my dear, sweet dog. Why couldn't he have slipped away peacefully, and on his own? Overcoming guilt has been my biggest challenge throughout the grieving process. I felt like I killed my dog. I wasn't able to comprehend that I really *had* made the best decision. I wasn't able to accept that euthanasia was the most humane way out of this and the one recommended by everyone on the veterinary team. I return again and again to his last day, when I watched the clock and counted down the time we had left together, when I had to take him on his last drive, to his last vet visit, to say my last goodbye. I ruminate over the "What if's . . . What if I had done A, B, or C? Would it have changed anything? Totally irrational thoughts ruled my brain. I'd forgotten how much he suffered and why I had to make this decision. There's no benefit in this thinking, I realize that, and it dug me deeper and deeper into a hole.

Three months after Knuckles' death, I found myself in a dark place, the darkest of all the places I've ever been. In that same time span, I had also lost my cousin and two of our childhood cats. I felt numb and, worse, I lost hope. What was the point of living? I was tired of loving and losing and tired of crying. I was just tired. My heart couldn't take any more loss. Not only did I think about dying, I thought about how I could end my life and even had a plan. I've been in dark places before but always had my animals to comfort me. This time, it was different: I had never experienced this level of hopelessness and despair. Knuckles was waiting for me on the other side, I knew it. I just wanted to be with him, that's all I wanted. At the time, nothing else mattered … I just needed my dog.

Swift intervention was needed. I kept thinking about what would happen to my birds and cats if I were gone. Surely no one would love them the same way I do; they know me, I know them, and we know exactly how to comfort each other. If I didn't have other animals around me at the time Knuckles had died, I'm afraid to think of what really might have happened. I know that I wouldn't be here writing my story. One tends to grieve and mourn in the same way that they love. In my case, it was intensely. Knuckles rocked my world coming in, and rocked it even harder when he left it. He affected my life so much that I could hardly remember the twenty-two years before him. It's like he'd always been there.

Before Knuckles' final journey, our veterinarian said something that will stay with me forever. "You love him so much that you're willing to take his pain away by giving it to yourself." I've never heard a truer statement. A close friend recently asked that if I had the choice to bring Knuckles back, would I? My first thought was, "Of course!" After remembering how much he had suffered during his last days, I reconsidered. Wanting to bring him back arose out of my desire to have him by my side more than anything. However, I didn't want him to relive one minute of his suffering.

Knuckles' death brought up a lot of unfinished mourning from my own life. I found myself revisiting other losses that had been pushed away and never addressed, such as childhood traumas, my marriage, my divorce, and other relationships that ended for one reason or another. Painful as it was, I began the hard work of confronting all of these and looking at the impact they had on my life and on my heart. At the recommendation of my therapist, I sought the help of a pet loss support group and found Beyond the Paw Print through an online search. I reached out to the facilitator, Micky Golden Moore, and began to attend the monthly meetings.

Beyond the Paw Print has been a blessing in my life. The monthly meetings have given me a safe place to share my story and my feelings, and to recognize that I did *the best* I could, providing for Knuckles throughout his entire life, including his final days. I've always had a deep connection and bond with animals and it's not often that I encounter others with similar feelings. My feelings felt validated and I discovered that I wasn't the only one experiencing this intense grief.

Prior to being a part of the group, I grieved in isolation, feeling disconnected from others who were moving on with their lives. While I now have a wonderful and supportive boyfriend, family, friends, and coworkers who understand, not everyone always knows how to provide comfort. Some well-meaning people still say or do things that hurt more than heal; or aren't comfortable talking about death. Unfortunately, I learned that there were some who didn't have my best interest at heart, and for my own well-being, I've had to remove them from my life.

Now, I look forward to my BTPP meetings as a time to reflect on my life with Knuckles, as well as to connect with the stories that others share about their beloved pets. No one judges anyone. We come together for the same purpose, to connect and heal.

It's easy for me to focus on the end of Knuckles' life and forget about the entire decade we had together before his decline. We had so many wonderful years together! Lately, I've been looking over all the photographs and videos taken of us and it's been cathartic. In Knuckles' memory, I made a hardcover photo book, purchased a beautiful sterling silver necklace engraved with his name on it, and on my arm, had a tattoo drawn of his portrait and paw print. Whenever the time is right, I'll lovingly welcome another dog into my home, and make sure to tell my new friend all about Knuckles.

Some days are easier to manage than others, but there's still not one that goes by where I don't think of my precious dog. I cannot say that time has made my loss any easier. What I can say about time is that it appears to have rounded off some of the sharper edges. I can't say with certainty how I will feel tomorrow, but today I can say that I'm OK. I visit Knuckles' grave often. He's buried near Bob and Baby, my two beloved childhood cats. I sit and talk with all of them, sharing our memories and telling them of all the wonderful things I loved about them. I always tell Knuckles how he was the best friend that I've ever had, and that one day we'll meet again, but this time, we'll be together for eternity.

SONNY

STORY ELEVEN

In My Heart Forever

By Jackie

IT WAS IN A NEARBY NEIGHBORHOOD that I had seen the sign: Chocolate Labrador puppies for sale. A full year had passed since I'd lost my beloved Bandit, and I'd started thinking about getting a new puppy. I talked to my sister about it, and she suggested we take a look. It was decided: We made a date to go see the puppies later that afternoon.

When the puppies saw us, they started leaping with excitement. What a sweet sight! There was one who remained calm though, unlike the rest. His quiet, easygoing personality amidst that puppy madness reminded me … of me. After holding him, there was only one decision to make, and it was the best decision ever. I met my Sonny on July 23, 2010.

This dog captured my heart from day one, and we were always together. Daily walks and regular visits to local dog parks were routine. When we were at home, Sonny followed me from room to room; he wanted to be wherever I was. He even accompanied me on all my vacations to Northern Michigan. Sonny was always there for me, as the non-judgmental, understanding ear I needed. I talked to him as I would to a person and believed that he understood. When I placed the chicken on top of his regular food and told him it was too hot to eat, he turned and walked away. After a few minutes, when the chicken had cooled off, I would tell him it was time to eat, at which time he'd join me in the kitchen to enjoy his meal.

In return, Sonny would also talk to me. When he wanted something, he would bark. I'd try to figure out what he wanted, and make sure he got it. When in receipt of that toy or treat, Sonny would then lay down. Sometimes, those special barks indicated that he wanted me to lay down on the floor with him or perform some other routine task. Sonny had me trained!

I was all too happy to accommodate his every need. Ours was a very special connection, so much so that people would often comment that they never saw a dog look at a person the way Sonny looked at me … with complete love and devotion, the same love and devotion I returned every day.

Everyone associated me with Sonny: at the dog park, on our walks, at the indoor dog swimming center, on social media, even my friends and family knew me as "Sonny's Mom." Marriage and children hadn't happened for me yet, but that was okay because Sonny was my family. I always told him that he was the love of my life. He was truly my soulmate.

When Sonny was seven, I noticed that he had a lump between his chest and stomach. I immediately contacted my veterinarian to set up an appointment. The doctor tested the lump and determined that it was non-cancerous; but recommended that we watch it and wait. As time passed, I decided to have it removed when I noticed a difference in Sonny's energy level. Something had changed with my boy and he was moving slower than normal. I firmly believed that after the lump was removed, he would return to his normal self.

In the midst of this decision, I learned that my veterinarian had moved to another practice. Because I'd been very happy with the treatment she'd provided for Sonny, I decided to follow her in order to retain continuity of care. She scheduled surgery to remove the lump in August 2017. Sonny had always been in good health, and neither of us had reason to believe there might be any complications.

I later found out that the owner of the practice, also a vet, had taken over Sonny's surgery when I was under the impression that my veterinarian would be the primary surgeon. My doctor unfortunately had to leave for the day right as Sonny went into recovery and wasn't there to observe him. I firmly believed my vet was going to be present to manage all aspects of Sonny's case, from beginning to end. Even now I become upset when I think of the course of events. When I picked Sonny up, the veterinary practice owner reported that he had done very well and had no concerns for his recovery. I took him home and never left his side.

Initially, everything seemed fine and appeared as if he was recovering normally. Then the unthinkable occurred: 24 hours later, Sonny laid down on the floor and never woke up. I saw him lay down behind the couch and thought it would be a good idea to let him rest for a while. I had no idea that anything might be wrong. When I checked on him a little later, I found him motionless on the floor. In my distress, I kept trying to wake him up. I continue to feel traumatized when I replay that moment of finding him. I couldn't accept it: the thought of losing my sweet dog made no sense. Just the day before, he was fine. I felt so much guilt. He had only been out of my sight for a brief amount of time.

I called my brother-in-law, who helped me get Sonny into the car and went with me to the emergency veterinary hospital. I told them to do everything they could. I was hoping for a miracle. It was like a scene from a movie — the movie you don't want to watch — when the doctor came out to the waiting room and told me they did everything they could, but Sonny hadn't made it. It was time to say goodbye.

The unimaginable had happened, and I was determined to learn what went wrong with this otherwise healthy dog. It just didn't make sense. I began my journey to review every single step of Sonny's care – from diagnosis through surgery, from one specialist to another. Through my investigation, I learned that Sonny had been released from the hospital prematurely. Even though my veterinarian had to leave, she was confident that he would receive excellent post-surgical care by the staff.

When I told others that Sonny was unable to walk out of the veterinary office after the surgery, they told me that their dogs had appeared alert and walked out easily after every surgery. I didn't realize that this might be unusual, thinking that his behavior was normal when anesthesia was involved. I trusted the team when they told me that he was fine to go home.

With further research, I discovered the following: Sonny was released too soon, just two hours after his four-hour surgery. In addition, excessive anesthesia and a fentanyl patch, all of which may have been too much for his body to manage, may have contributed to his premature death. I also learned that the practice was preparing to close for the evening and was not staffed sufficiently to keep him overnight. Unfortunately, I wasn't directed to take him to an emergency facility, where he could have been observed overnight. Though I was in the midst of grief, I kept digging and moving forward. Nothing would stop me from finding out what happened to my sweet boy.

Soon thereafter, I filed a complaint with our state's Department of Licensing and Regulatory Affairs, which led to an investigation. The investigator gathered information and interviews from all involved. During this process, they also discovered that Sonny's surgery took longer than anticipated, hence the extra medications to keep him sedated.

The investigator warned me that the process may take up to a year before an outcome would be determined. Ultimately my goal was to have this veterinary practice recognize the errors that led to my dog's death and to never allow them to be repeated. More than anything though, I would rather have my dog back. Prior to the publication of this book, I learned that Sonny's case had been closed, with no violations found. As you can imagine, I was extremely distressed and heartbroken at this, and very frustrated to learn that after such an in-depth investigation, the outcome determined no wrongdoing.

As I reflect on all of these events, I continue to be weighed down by feelings of guilt over Sonny's death. I retrace the events of his final hours over and over in my mind. I wish I could go back in time, knowing what I know now. I recall how I said and did unreasonable things like bargain with God and anyone listening, willing to do anything to have him back. Sonny was only seven and I had anticipated many fun years ahead.

Before his surgery, I had started a new job, which would have allowed us much more time together. I felt cheated by his premature passing. My friends, family, and his dog friends, everyone he loved and who loved him, were also cheated. I still have trouble making sense of it. He was an innocent, gentle animal, and deserved so much more. My distress has made my grief difficult to process. Every decision I made during Sonny's life was in his best interest. I was his protector, but I continue to think about all the events that led to his untimely death and how, that one time, I couldn't protect him.

I learned about Beyond the Paw Print Pet Loss Support Group from a friend on Facebook. Attending the monthly meetings has been life-changing for me. It's a safe haven where I can say anything without being judged. In fact, many who attend relate to my stories and the feelings I share. From the first meeting, I felt a strong connection with everyone there. I learned that I wasn't alone in my grief.

That's because many of the people in our lives don't want to hear about our grief or don't know what to say. Fortunately, I do have people I can talk to, but there are others who don't want to hear about it anymore. My comfort comes from BTPP meetings. Everyone in the group has been warm and welcoming. We're all going through the same thing and they have helped me work through my emotions. Dr. Micky Golden Moore, who founded BTPP, is an absolute Godsend.

As I move forward in my new normal, there are ways I've kept Sonny's memory alive. I've donated to a variety of dog rescue organizations in his memory. I let myself, hard as it is, think about him and talk about him. I dream of opening a doggie daycare and naming it after Sonny. I often made special dog treats for my boy, which is something I'd like to include in a daycare – a dog-friendly store with a human and canine menu. If I won the lottery, I would love to have a sanctuary and help save animals.

There is not a day that goes by that I don't think about Sonny. I have moved from constant crying to having good and bad days. My grief is sometimes overwhelming and some days, my heart *physically* hurts. The pain is unbearable at times, and often results in bouts of anxiety or depression. I've also discovered that certain activities trigger my grief; a walk in my neighborhood, sitting on my deck, or trips to Northern Michigan. This also applies to the firsts without Sonny: the first time I visited a close friend and her dogs; the first year celebrating holidays and birthdays; and now the first anniversary of the day he died. It is still *so hard* to believe that he is gone.

It has been a little over a year, but I still talk to Sonny, and I know he's there. I dream about him, and I also receive signs from him. His side of the bed remains empty, but I have felt him jumping up and laying against me in my sleep. One time, when I felt his presence, I woke up and discovered one of my socks on my pillow. I don't know where it came from, but Sonny liked to lay on my clothes. He was leaving me a sign.

At one of the meetings, a BTPP member shared the experience he had with a pet communicator. I was intrigued and decided to make an appointment. Although there are those who find this form of communication unconventional or improbable, I believe in it. There wasn't anything I wouldn't try in order to connect with Sonny. The communicator and I corresponded via email, and yes, even with this limited contact, the experience was nothing short of amazing. She shared specific stories about our lives together and described in detail the dogs that I've loved and lost. I was told that they were present, as was my dad (whom she described in detail) to greet Sonny at the time of his passing.

She also told me that if I saw a bunny, it would be a sign that Sonny was nearby. During his lifetime, bunnies would often venture into our yard, seemingly unafraid of my sweet but sizable dog. I think they sensed that he wouldn't hurt them. Perhaps they recognized that Sonny was a gentle soul. Since my reading with the pet communicator, I've seen bunnies unexpectedly, at odd times, in unusual places, especially during rough moments when I've been grieving over Sonny. On one occasion, I saw a rabbit with her baby. When I stopped to watch them, she came closer and just sat and looked at me. It was truly special.

Through this loss, I have learned that life can change in an instant. I could never have imagined that a routine surgery would result in Sonny's death and force me to adjust to life without my best friend. He was my heart, my soul, my love. I have learned something very valuable as a result of this experience; to live as our dogs live, enjoying every healthy moment. Treat them as they treat you; with complete joy and love. It will still break your heart when they leave, but you'll have all the special memories to cherish. It helps to know that they are always with you, just in a different way.

Everyone has their own unique journey through grief. Take care of yourself and do what's right for you. Don't be afraid to go to a support group, or individual therapy, if it's what you need. No one knows what's right for you, only you do. Some people adopt a new pet right away, some wait, and some choose never to adopt again. Everyone's experience is unique. One day I'll be ready to give love to another dog – there are so many in need. I love you and I miss you Sonny. You are in my heart forever. Until we meet again . . .

HANA

STORY TWELVE

One Last Time

By Mary Anne

IT WAS FITTING THAT MY GORGEOUS and glamorous kitty was born in the land of beautiful people, Los Angeles, California. Hana was adopted by my son Chris, who had made the Golden State his home after leaving Michigan several years ago. He loved her beautiful Calico coloring, the black, white, orange, and light brown, and her gorgeous big eyes, which were a shade of green that appeared to change color depending on the light. Visiting Chris was something I did frequently which gave me the opportunity to become acquainted with young Hana, whom I found irresistible.

Several months after adopting her, Chris had to move, due to circumstances beyond his control, and was unable to find an apartment that allowed cats. He called and asked if I would consider adopting Hana. I instantly said yes. My twelve-year-old, gentle cat, Keety, had recently received her angel wings and although I thought about waiting longer to adopt again, I was determined to provide Hana with a home she could call her own.

Chris made arrangements for Hana to be flown to Michigan with Tonnie, a family friend who happened to be visiting her daughter in Los Angeles at the time. Tonnie agreed to shepherd Hana home safely inside her new carrier, with a veterinary-prescribed tranquilizer to help keep her calm in flight. I greeted the two of them at the airport, so excited to bring this beautiful cat home.

When we arrived, I carefully took Hana into the kitchen and slowly unzipped the carrier while speaking gentle words of encouragement. She gingerly stepped out, puzzled by her new surroundings, and explored every nook and cranny. Our eyes locked, and it was love at first sight. I believe Hana sensed, on some level, my connection to Chris and recognized me from my visits. She knew we weren't total strangers.

Because I realized that cats like to stare out the window, I installed a kitty seat under the windowsill in the den. I kept the blinds there for privacy, closing them in the evening and opening them up again every morning. Peeking through the slats became Hana's favorite activity. In the morning, she would follow me around, making it clear that she wanted the slats open. She loved to watch the squirrels, rabbits, and woodchucks, as well as the people walking their dogs. There were always an astonishing number of feathered friends sitting on the windowsill, teasing her without mercy.

Hana was delighted when she discovered the many comfy kitty beds I had placed throughout the house. Her favorite place was by the heat register in the living room, a chosen spot during the cold winter months. She loved to sleep on my bed too, on top of my large white satin quilt. Hana woke me up every morning by pressing her sweet pink nose on mine and licking my nose until I was fully awake. Her message was loud and clear: "Wake up mommy. I'm hungry!"

One day in 1996, after many years of living with kidney disease, I had to succumb to dialysis. I was one of the rare patients who had to wait only two years to receive a donor kidney. The turn of events meant I was in and out of the hospital for six weeks as a result of complications from surgery. Throughout my recovery,

Hana sensed what was going on. Prior to all of this, she would jump on my stomach, curl into a ball, and fall asleep. In my newly convalescent state, she somehow knew that her usual course of action wouldn't be allowable, on my stomach or anywhere else on my body. Instead, she jumped onto my bed, circled me three or four times, and then laid down beside me. Hana did this whenever the nurse or others came for a visit. I believe it was her way of protecting me.

My girl was fortunate enough to enjoy a long and happy life, nearly fourteen years, until she developed rheumatoid arthritis. Activities that used to come naturally, such as jumping onto the couch, became increasingly difficult. To compensate, I placed one of her favorite beds on the floor next to mine. As the disease progressed and she was no longer able to chase the chipmunks in the yard, she still appeared happy to watch their antics from her window seat. Hana adored being outside, but as walking became more difficult, I would carry her to the garden so she could relax. I would lay her favorite quilt down by the creek, and together, we would listen to the birds sing and watch the fish swim by. Sometimes, I sat on the garden bench nearby, penning stories and poetry while keeping a close watch on my precious sweet girl. Now and then, Hana would make a gallant yet unsuccessful attempt at walking, trying to crawl toward a curious chipmunk, and sadly, I would place her back on her quilt. I could tell she enjoyed being in this world with me, but it was very hard to watch her struggle. I just wasn't ready to say goodbye.

As she became increasingly ill, and struggled with bladder and bowel control, it was important for me to keep to a strict schedule for Hana. My son John was a tremendous help. He came to my home every evening and assisted me in her care. We gave Hana a warm bath every night and she had the pleasure of being blown dry afterward. She loved it, especially when we wrapped her up in a big heated towel at the end. Despite her struggles, Hana continued to enjoy her favorite foods, especially salmon. She had other choices and it wouldn't have surprised me if she could read the labels. Hana was ever-aware and ever-intelligent, but we had to keep a close eye on her weight, or it would aggravate her illness.

As autumn set in, Hana stayed on the unheated sun porch. She slept on a clean rug every night with a fresh kitty pad nearby in case she had to relieve herself. I placed an old metal hat rack with a heat lamp attached overhead so she could be as warm as possible. At 10:00 p.m. every night, I gave Hana another of her favorite treats, a small can of tuna. Cozy and comfortable, and with a full tummy, she always slept soundly. She appeared comfortable with this routine, which led me to believe we had time to make more memories together.

A few months later, I learned that my eldest son, Ken, had become ill after a serious operation. Ken lived in New York and needed help to care for Claire, his four-year-old daughter. Now I needed help since I was uncertain of how long I'd be away. I had to find someone with a flexible schedule who could, and would, lovingly care for my aging girl. It was then that I remembered my nephew Bill, who knew and loved Hana very much. Bill jumped at the chance to take care of "Baby Girl" as he called her. Since he was a bachelor, he was able to move into my home, a perfect solution – or so I thought.

I gave Bill a detailed copy of Hana's schedule and feedings, with the expectation that he would closely follow them. Two days later, he called me from the vet's office. Bill had followed my schedule to the letter, except for giving Hana her nightly portion of tuna. In recounting the story, Bill told me that 10:00 p.m. had been too late for him to stay up, so he went to bed thirty minutes earlier, without providing her nightly treat. Bill woke to find Hana painfully wedged between the door and a chair. She had been trying to leave the porch and get to the kitchen for one of the few things that made her happy.

I've gone over the scene a million times in my head. *Why didn't he just give her the treat at 9:30 p.m.?* Hana had suffered for hours being stuck undiscovered, so much so that our vet recommended she be laid to rest. I let out an anguished cry. If an X-ray had been taken of my heart at that moment, it would have shown a crack right through the center. I could not believe I would never see my Hana again. The pain I felt was unbearable. Since I was still in New York, I asked the vet to cremate Hana. I didn't want her buried, but wanted her by my side, always. Hana was seventeen years old when she crossed the Rainbow Bridge.

When I returned to Michigan, I read an article in the local newspaper about Micky Golden Moore, the founder of Beyond the Paw Print. The first meeting was going to be held on the second Monday in March 2009. By that time, Hana had been gone for six months, but I was still grieving terribly, and knew I needed help. The grief and guilt over the way my beloved girl had lived out her final days was overwhelming. I attended that very first meeting of BTPP with the hope that it would be a gathering of animal lovers who, like me, were feeling great emotion over their loss, and where I would receive consolation in a confidential environment. This was just what I needed to release the pain over losing my sweet Hana. However, I realized one meeting was not sufficient.

Sleep was incredibly difficult, and I still spent many hours crying, and even hallucinated that Hana was on my bed. Surprisingly, when I attended the next meeting, I found that the number of those in attendance had increased. I didn't realize that so many others were suffering, too. So many broken hearts, so much grieving. As each person took a turn going through their story, I understood that this was where I needed to be at that moment. We were all in the same boat, sharing our pain and helping each other in the process. BTPP helped me to feel a little less brokenhearted and to recognize that Hana would be alive in my heart and mind forever.

I will never understand why it's so hard to understand people like us, meaning those who have a strong connection with their animals and experience profound grief over their loss. I will never forget how my employer laughed when one of my colleagues brought me a card and bouquet of flowers, and said, "That's the stupidest thing I've ever heard anyone doing, over the death of a cat!"

Thanks to the support group attendees, and especially Micky, losing Hana was easier to manage. Because of unfortunate and numerous medical problems, meetings became increasingly difficult for me to attend. Every word of comfort, along with the love and fellowship found at those meetings, will never leave my heart and soul. Sharing my sorrow and pain, and knowing others understood, was what I needed. God bless all of you for your kindness to me and to each other.

I didn't think I could possibly love another cat or dog again, but my inner voice kept nagging at me: I *have* to get somebody. My son John and I eventually started visiting shelters, looking, holding, and touching little faces until I realized what I was doing; I was looking for Hana! Perhaps I just wasn't ready. As we were leaving the very last shelter, I felt compelled to turn around. There was a tiger kitty with an exceptionally cute face stretched out and looking over her shoulder.

I went to the cage and lifted her out. She was three years old, and due to be put down in three days. Not on my watch! I named her Evita. In my lifetime, I've had cats, dogs, and even three baby chicks as pets, but Evita was the smartest one yet. I truly believe she was a little girl in a cat's body. She loved her treats and naturally wanted more than the limited daily allotment. All by herself, Evita figured out how to open the treat door. She was never boring: Evita's antics kept me fully entertained!

After five wonderful years together, I became too weak to care for Evita properly, so my older sister, Ramona, who lives in Florida, offered to adopt her. I still felt motivated to do something that would honor both of my cats, so I decided to put my energy toward charitable causes with animals at their heart. I became a member of our local Humane Society and a variety of animal rights and rescue organizations. I'm eighty-six years old and still counting.

I urge all of you to get your own somebody from a shelter; it won't be a replacement for your great loss, but will be somebody for you to love and who will love you back. I do hope you will make that decision. I miss Hana every day, but accept that in my remaining time on earth, I will demonstrate my love for animals from afar and continue to find an outlet through my poetry. I wrote the following poem in memory of Hana:

One Last Time
By Mary Anne

Losing Hana without holding her,
one last time.
Without feeling her beautiful multi-colored coat,
one last time.
Without her soft body next to mine,
one last time.
Without kissing her little pink nose,
one last time.

JACKSON & CRAWFORD

STORY THIRTEEN

Snaughty Boys

By Jake (a.k.a. Lori)

"I WANT THIS KITTY," I SAID to my husband John, who responded with a sidelong glance that could only be interpreted as, "*What* are you doing?" We met Jackson, a six-month-old rescue, at a veterinary hospital near our home. The handsome boy was decked out in a fluffy tuxedo, and had a long black coat that contrasted with his stunning white bib, white belly and paws, with a streak of white fur right down his nose. The stunning waif of a cat strutted toward me with his tail held high. I scooped him up and he proceeded to press the top of his head underneath my chin as though we were long lost friends. What a lover! I was smitten. A few weeks later, our family grew with a new addition.

Jackson, named by the vet who rescued him, adjusted easily to his new life in our home and was comfortable from the start with our two dogs. I learned that tuxedo cats have a larger-than-life personality. This was true of our new boy: He wanted to be the boss and poke his nose into everyone else's business. He always smelled like fresh laundry. I know because I would bury my nose in his side and inhale deeply. Jackson was so popular we even had people offer to buy him! No amount of money, though, no matter how large, could make us part with our lovely kitty.

Jackson's front paws were our only frustration with an otherwise perfect cat. They were declawed, a practice I vehemently disagree with, and one I believe contributed to the reason he became a chewer. It didn't take long to discover that he'd chew and bite most anything, including electrical cords, shoes, eyeglasses, dish towels and boxes. He destroyed more expensive items than my dogs! We had Jackson's teeth checked several times and there was nothing wrong with them. Without claws, he used the only other sharp objects he had to compensate.

John and I became skilled at trying to preempt Jackson from chewing valuables. He was a terror around electrical cords, which was frightening. If it looked like he was about to chew on something, we would scold him or yell, "Jackson, no!" and he'd look up at our faces, his pink bottom lip sticking out slightly. It was so adorable that I could never stay upset with him. However, whenever he wasn't happy with us, he conveyed his feelings directly … If he was fast asleep and one of us sneezed loudly, he would raise his head and make a whining sound of disgust, often with his eyes closed, as if to say, "Keep it down people!"

About a year after adopting Jackson, I was visiting a feline-only veterinary practice and the technicians brought out a tiny brown tabby kitten found abandoned on a construction site. They were hoping I might be interested in adopting the eight-week old sweetie; I was, and I did! I named him Crawford.

From the very start, Jackson was smitten with his new brother. He loved and cared for this kitten in every way imaginable. The feeling was mutual. Crawford followed him everywhere. We loved watching Jackson take his big fluffy paws and push Crawford to the ground in order to scrub him with his pink tongue from head to toe. Crawford wriggled and screamed but was pinned to the ground for his daily bath. As the years went by, they formed a wonderful bond. They ate together, played together, napped together, bathed one another, and loved to curl up in one another's arms.

Crawford was an adorable short-haired tabby and became my right-hand man. Every morning, he stretched out on my lap making a deep rumbling purr while I enjoyed my daily hot water and honey. Part of our routine was the kiss I laid on the special marking that formed an "m" on the top of his head. When it came time to make coffee, he would jump on the counter and sit and watch while I poured water into the canister and prepared the filter and grounds. After I placed the grounds into the coffee pot, he performed a most amazing feat: Crawford walked behind the pot and rubbed against it, while his tail went under the lid and flipped it shut. This became our daily routine for years, and I treasured it immensely.

This cat was sweetness personified, and liked everyone, human or animal. When we traveled to visit my parents, we took our animals, which included our Irish setter, Ilsa, and both cats. Crawford was always happy to see my parents' orange tabbies, McDougal and Murphy. Jackson though was the opposite and spent the first 24 hours hissing and growling. He calmed down soon enough, only to take over the whole group. My kitties were a continuous source of entertainment. My sister, who also adored them, gave them the nickname "snaughty boys," a combination of silly and naughty. Life was good.

In June 2015, a chain of events began that, as it unfolded, was a struggle to comprehend. On June 11, we made the decision to euthanize our thirteen-year-old Irish setter, Ilsa, who had multiple health issues. After one particularly bad day that resulted in two grand mal seizures, we knew that it was time for our vet to help end her suffering. Rather than leave her body at the veterinary hospital, where arrangements could be made for the crematorium to retrieve her, we chose a different way to say goodbye.

Our Farewell Journey, as we call it, started with Ilsa and is now a part of how we say goodbye to all of our animals. Although not for everybody, it works for us. We brought Ilsa's body home to "lie in state" so that our entire animal family could see her and say goodbye. We placed her on a favorite bed in the family room, surrounded by her toys, played soft music, said some prayers, and spent time reminiscing and in quiet reflection. I clipped a snippet of her beautiful red hair to keep with me, too. The next morning, we personally delivered Ilsa's body to the crematorium. My intention was to handle my dog with the reverence she deserved. Her ashes are now housed in a beautiful wooden box, along with the lock of her hair. Our farewell journey has become a meaningful and important way to honor the lives of the animals we have loved.

Most importantly, we hope that our special practice of saying goodbye helps our other animals discern that their companion has died. It's important that they have an opportunity to see their deceased family member and say goodbye too, rather than have them simply disappear one day and never return.

Seven days after we said goodbye to Ilsa, my car was rear-ended while stopped at a red light on my way to work. The accident further injured my already-challenged spine. Fourteen days after that, I received a phone call that my father had died unexpectedly. Along with our animals, we drove four hours to be with my mom. Our stay was exhausting, but meaningful. We were just thinking we could breathe a little and returned to visit my mom for Thanksgiving, when my husband received a call from his sister that their mom was dying. We rushed home and fortunately, he was able to see her before she passed away.

In the most unbelievable chain of events, two months later, my mom's kidney function declined dramatically. She refused dialysis, and made the decision, on her own, to enter hospice. I felt like I had fallen from the frying pan right into the fire. Nothing seemed to be able to stop the conveyor belt of death. I took a leave of absence from work and moved in with my mother.

My mom was a nurse and had spent her life taking care of others, but now it was my turn to be her caregiver. Though I had cared for many ailing animals, and had been present when they passed away, I had never done the same with a human being. I prayed I would be capable of providing the care my mom needed. We had some amazing conversations during that time and without hesitation, I can say it was a privilege, even though it was one of the hardest things I have ever done. She wanted to die in the comfort of her home and not in a cold, sterile hospital. I'm grateful that I was able to honor her request.

Mom's beloved orange tabby, McDougal, slept in the hospital bed with her. McDougal's younger brother, Murphy, was frightened of the equipment and visitors and remained out of sight until the house fell quiet. The first night that I arrived, Mom sat me down and told me that I wouldn't like what she had to say, *but that I must listen*. Her final wish was that we euthanize Murphy and McDougal. She was distressed at the thought of them being removed at their ages, from the only home they had ever known. When mom told me about her decision for Murphy and McDougal, I was reeling. I felt sick, frightened, conflicted, and confused as I listened to my mom's unexpected final wish. They were not just someone's cats; they were members of my family. McDougal had shown up as a stray and Murphy was a gift from me to my dad when he was depressed during his recovery from open-heart surgery. The conveyor belt of death was running so fast, I felt I was being buried alive.

The months following the deaths of my dad, both our moms, Murphy, and McDougal, were beyond difficult. In many ways I was just surviving, putting one foot in front of another. In the midst of these losses, our cat Jackson started exhibiting symptoms that required our attention. In early 2017, an ultrasound revealed diffuse lymphoma; he had cancer in the lining of his intestine. This was my third cat with lymphoma … only this time there was no solid tumor to remove. We pursued holistic treatment, and for a while, he responded.

In the midst of our losses, we were also taking care of John's Uncle Richie, a shy, smart, and sweet Korean War veteran who never married, and had no family of his own. Eventually, as his health declined, John moved Richie into an assisted living facility, where he appeared to thrive. One month later, though, he was rushed to the hospital with severe abdominal pain and died.

Just a few weeks after Richie's death, our cat Jackson appeared to be losing ground to the cancer that had struck him. One morning when I went to lift him up for his daily regimen, Jackson vocalized his discomfort with low, deep moans, as if to say, "No thank you, I don't want to do this anymore." Hearing those noises showed me the depth of his pain. The anguish in my soul was beyond comprehension. I was overcome by the gravity of the situation. I could deny it no longer. Jackson was ready to say goodbye.

While I prepared to call to our vet's office to make arrangements for Jackson's final visit, I noticed Crawford was sitting on the counter waiting for me. He didn't look good. He had refused breakfast, and had thrown up a small amount of clear liquid. His eyes were at half-mast, and the hair on his back was sticking out. He did not close the lid on the coffee maker as usual. That night, I took Crawford with us to the vet's office, knowing something was wrong. Before we said goodbye to Jackson, our vet gave Crawford an exam and drew blood. The compassionate vet technicians at our practice kept Crawford company in a separate room, which allowed us to concentrate on being with Jackson for this final act of love.

We brought Jackson's body home to lie-in-state on his favorite bed, repeating our ritual of music, prayers and quiet reflection. After our other animals had time to sense that their friend had passed, we delivered Jackson's body to the crematorium. Throughout the day, Crawford was very quiet. I worried intensely about how I might help him adjust to life without Jackson. My vet called in the morning with test results: Crawford had pancreatitis and required fluids to keep him hydrated along with an anti-nausea remedy. The vet said if Crawford wasn't better the following morning, take him to the emergency clinic. The next morning, he had not improved, so I promptly took him to the ER where the vet performed an ultrasound.

A few hours later I received a phone call that I will never forget. "I have been practicing medicine for 20 years and have never seen anything like this," the doctor said. "The ultrasound showed his pancreas and liver are full of cancer." The room shrank and I had trouble breathing. I could not comprehend what was being said. The words were inconceivable. I was struggling to stay on this side of sanity. The "one more thing," that I said I could not handle was bearing down on me like a tornado out of control.

The conveyor belt of death was on high speed. I would do anything, offer anything, and change everything to make this not be true. Over and over, I needed to know how Crawford could be dying? Where did this come from? Why did I not see any signs? How could I have missed something so serious?"

There was nothing to do but return to the animal clinic. In the time I had been gone, Crawford had deteriorated. Apparently, his intent was to leave this earth and be with Jackson, who had received his angel wings just 48 hours earlier. Death would not separate these two, who were soul mates in every way. Who was I to say it was unfair? If ever I needed my right-hand man, Crawford, it was now, to help me process the loss of eight family members, but this was not to be. We had another lie-in-state ceremony, this time, for Crawford.

Our vet told us about a pet loss support group run by Dr. Micky Golden Moore called Beyond the Paw Print. I found Micky's website and contacted her with the subject line, "drowning in grief."

She was very kind and spoke with me a few times on the phone, until I was able to attend a monthly meeting. It's an emotional experience listening to others tell their story, but somehow comforting to know I am not the only person going through such deep sorrow. Micky strives to keep the meeting on track and allow everyone an opportunity to talk. As hard as it is to tell this story, and to sob in front of complete strangers, I have to admit that the process is cathartic. When it was over, I felt strengthened, empowered, and most of all *seen and heard*. Micky has been a tremendous source of support, always available outside the meetings, warmly offering support or additional resources. She is a treasure!

I have struggled to make sense of this nightmare, to make sense of all of these losses. The only way I survived in those months, after losing nine members of my family in a two-year period, was to encase myself in some kind of mythical armor. It was the only way I could guard myself from the pain. But this strategy resulted in a terrifying health crisis and hospitalization about eight months after Crawford died. I'm now working on peeling back the layers of grief and learning how not addressing it took a tremendous toll on my mind and my body. Part of that work is seeing a therapist who specializes in grief and a physician who studies the connection between our mind, our thoughts, and our physical body. Meditation and practicing mindfulness have also entered the fold. The loving support of a wonderful husband has also been a huge part of my trip back. Additionally, I have donated to local and national animal rescues, in memory of my boys. When I'm feeling better, I intend to enlarge my memorial garden in the back yard with special flowers and memorial stones.

There are two things that have helped lighten my heavy heart: A year and a half after enduring the loss of nine family members, John and I adopted a pair of six-month old male kittens. I refer to them as "salve for a broken heart." These two tightly bonded siblings, Weston (a ginger and white) and Price (a silver tabby) are slowly integrating themselves into the family and getting used to our dogs, Brookfield, an English Springer Spaniel, and an Irish setter named Hunter. They have brought joy and happiness to our hearts. The kitties make me laugh every day with their underage antics. Their need for love, affection, and nurturing are a balm to my soul. I am thrilled to be a new mama again.

DANNY

STORY FOURTEEN

Love at First Sight

By Jill

HAVING A DOG IS LIKE HAVING A CHILD: a huge responsibility, a long-term commitment, and one that sometimes comes with unique and unexpected needs. When my daughter Rachel was nearing college age, and my son Jordan had started high school, the idea of adopting a dog became more realistic. Both of our children were born with asthma so when they were little, the doctor told us insistently, "No pets!" I had grown up with cats, and my husband, Mitchell, had grown up with dogs. I knew secretly he really wanted to get another, and deep down, I really wanted to have a new furry friend as well.

The summer before Rachel went off to college, Jordan and I got on the computer to look at adoptable dogs on various rescue sites and shelters. One shelter in particular drew our attention, because they accepted dogs from other shelters nearby when they had reached capacity. We were intrigued and made an appointment for a visit.

It was a warm day when we drove to the shelter, and we could already see the kennels from the parking area. One of the attendants greeted us warmly, sensing our excitement, and didn't waste a minute in getting us in front of the dogs. When she opened the kennel, Danny was the first to run out. He charged ahead of the others and right up to our son. It was love at first sight for all of us.

Danny was an adorable, skinny, two-year-old Dalmatian. We decided to keep his name, given by his original owner, an older woman who found herself unable to care for an active young dog. The staff members couldn't reveal much about Danny's current health condition. He had recently arrived from another shelter, just four days prior to our meeting him. We were about to find out.

We brought Danny home near the end of July 2001 and took him to the vet the next day. We suspected he had kennel cough, not unusual for rescues, but it turned out he actually had pneumonia, requiring X-rays and a double dose of antibiotics. Danny also needed a Bronchodilator, a liquid medication administered with a dropper that opened the air passages in his lungs. For the next few weeks, our Danny was a very sick boy. He had twice-weekly re-checks with the vet, and although he was a good patient, he was always very nervous, shedding quite a bit from shaking so hard. We nursed our puppy back to health, albeit with a hefty price tag, but we didn't care. We were madly in love with our new family member.

Danny was a sweet, lovable dog with *lots* of energy. He loved long walks and was very popular with all our neighborhood canines. He also loved car rides, especially to Grandma's house. Dalmatians tend to be high-strung, and we also discovered that our dog had some separation anxiety, especially when we first rescued him. While we were at work during the day, Danny found a number of ways to express his stress. He actually took a bite out of the first step of our oak staircase – no joke. Although we repaired it, you can still see the outline of his mouth in the wood. One time he scraped the wall in the dining room with his teeth and pulled off some drywall. Another time he chewed up our daughter's black leather belt, and regurgitated pieces of leather for the next few days. He did leave us the belt buckle, along with a $600 vet bill for stomach X-rays and medication.

Danny's shenanigans were just part of his charm. I loved him deeply, despite the domestic disturbances. I started collecting anything Dalmatian-themed: mugs, treat jars, photo frames, salt and pepper shakers, and much more. Family and friends were always looking for Dalmatian collectibles to add to our collection.

One summer day in 2010, we noticed a swelling on the side of Danny's face. Initially, we thought he had been bitten by something, but he seemed to be having trouble swallowing, as if he couldn't open his jaw fully. The vet took X-rays, but they weren't conclusive, so exploratory surgery was needed. The news wasn't good: He had a tumor in his throat that was likely cancerous. We were referred to an oncologist — a cancer specialist. Our vet was very kind and compassionate in her attempt to soften the news, but we were heartbroken.

We made an appointment immediately to see the oncologist that our vet recommended. Tests confirmed our worst fears: Danny did indeed have cancer. The oncologist explained that he wasn't a candidate for surgery, but in his case, the treatment plan required radiation. Although they had good results from this course of action, there were no guarantees. We immediately opted to do everything we could to save our baby.

Radiation wasn't easy for Danny, but toward the end of the treatments his appetite improved, and he became more playful. These happy results lasted about a month, and then his health began to deteriorate. Danny started bleeding from his mouth and was having trouble eating and swallowing. We returned to the oncologist and they discovered the cancer had spread. Danny was dying. We discussed euthanasia with the oncologist, but decided we wanted to take Danny home for the night.

We were literally in shock. He was suffering and we couldn't bear to see him like that. As long as it was in our power to help, his suffering had to end. There was no question we needed to do the most loving thing we could for Danny. We held him all night, and early the following morning we went to our regular vet's office, thinking that it would be better for Danny to be with the veterinary group who knew him the best. We were lucky that the office was only a quarter of a mile from our house, because we could barely see to drive through the tears. Everyone at the vet's office was wonderful, so kind and considerate. Danny died in our loving arms on Saturday, December 11, 2010. He was at peace; his suffering was over.

We stayed and held our boy for about an hour after he died. We decided to have him buried in a group grave with other dogs, so he wouldn't be alone. We feel comforted knowing that Danny had crossed over the Rainbow Bridge, the heavenly place all our pets are said to traverse when they pass into the next world.

We donated Danny's leftover medications — the heartworm, and flea and tick preventatives — to our vet's office. A large river rock sits on our fireplace hearth, engraved with the words "Danny, Forever in Our Hearts." The grief that followed was beyond anything I had ever experienced. I could not get out of bed for two days. We were all in so much pain. My husband went to work in a raging blizzard because he just couldn't stand being home without Danny. I was teaching at the time, but the schools were closed that Monday and Tuesday, because of the snow. It was, ironically, a fortunate occurrence.

I decided that we needed help coming to terms with our grief. After a few phone calls and an internet search, I found Dr. Micky Golden Moore of Beyond the Paw Print. I called Micky and left a message, and a little while later, she called me back. I poured my heart out, right there on the phone. I felt an immediate kinship as Micky listened with compassion and validated my feelings. During that conversation, she invited us to the next meeting.

Beyond the Paw Print saved us! Mitchell and I were able to talk about Danny and cry with people who truly understood our pain. There was no judgment, just love and kindness. We connected immediately with everyone in attendance. Many friendships developed as we shared our grief and listened with compassion through each of the stories that were shared. BTPP is unique in that everyone in the group understands the loving family connection that exists between pets and humans. As the facilitator, Micky, motivated by her own losses, respects that connection, and validates our need to grieve openly and without fear of judgment.

BTPP brings people from all walks of life together. We share a common bond. There is nothing better than a group of people who can support each other in their time of need. We found it refreshing to be with those who understood what it meant to lose a beloved pet, a four-footed child. When I showed Micky the scrapbook I had created of Danny's life, she suggested that I share it with the other attendees. Some people make scrapbooks of special times with their human family members; I had done that too! Mine illuminated all of the special moments in our dog's life. I had started the scrapbook when he was just a pup, so as you can imagine, there was lots of memorabilia between the covers. I included pictures of his dog friends as well as his people friends. I scanned Danny's collar, tags, and his favorite treats and added them to a page. Unexpectedly, many of the attendees were inspired by what I had created. I was glad that I could offer a tangible project that brought comfort to our BTPP family — especially in the hopes that it might help others. This special scrapbook holds the cherished memories of the time we spent with our precious dog.

Grief is an emotion everyone feels at some point during their lives. When a person dies, others understand readily why friends and family are grieving. When a pet dies, friends and family often do not understand the depth of the loss. This lack of understanding leads people to feel isolated, which just intensifies the grief. For many, the loss of a pet is like the loss of a child. Some pet parents are single, and their pets *are* their family. Married or single, partners or friends, we all grieve for our pets.

I believe that BTPP helped us move forward so we could rescue again. The meetings allowed us to connect with other kindred spirits, each of whom served an important role in our healing experience. We will always treasure the support we received and the reassurance that our grief was normal.

In time, we were able to open our hearts and rescue another dog. Our new companion is named Ozzie, and he came into our lives about a year after Danny had passed. Ozzie is a Dalmatian/Labrador/Bulldog mix, with black and white spots and markings that are similar to Danny's, yet slightly different. Although we were still dealing with our loss, we felt strongly about needing to rescue another dog. Ozzie had been housed by a local rescue shelter at an area pet supply store, having been returned to the shelter when he was only a year old. The family who owned him couldn't handle his high energy and his behavioral issues. We knew Danny would want us to save another dog, one with behavioral issues too, and give him a loving and permanent place to call home. We believe it was meant to be!

CHELSEA

STORY FIFTEEN

My Blizzard Birthday Baby

By Charlene

Two miracles occurred on a cold and snowy Friday evening in January, eighteen years ago. My husband was late coming home from work when our city was being deluged by a blizzard. The snow was coming down fast and furious, and I was worried sick about his safety. After calling him several times and getting no answer, my worry and fear got the better of me, and I started imagining terrible scenarios. He finally burst through the door. A miracle! I was so happy, *and* relieved that he was home. I could breathe again! Gratitude, however, was accompanied by frustration: Why hadn't he responded to my calls?

I soon learned why: He pulled his right arm from behind his back to reveal a ball of fur sitting in the palm of his hand, a champagne-colored puppy dotted with a few brown spots. My husband handed her to me and said, "Happy Birthday baby!" Miracle number two!

I was overcome with joy and love for this darling little puppy. We had been without a dog for nearly fifteen years, and my husband couldn't have chosen a better gift: A puppy to love and care for. My husband and I have children and grandchildren whom we love dearly. After becoming empty-nesters though, I'd talked about looking for a dog to add to our newly quiet household. We named this beautiful Bichon Shih Tzu mix Chelsea. Welcoming Chelsea to our home was a true blessing, and I thanked God for bringing us together.

There was so much emotion at that moment that I almost forgot about the awful blizzard bearing down outside. I took Chelsea from my husband's hand and he began to tell me her story. He had spoken with a local breeder after finding out that I had fallen in love with a Bichon Shih Tzu mix whom I had often seen walking with its owner in our subdivision. My husband told me that the breeder revealed she had two puppies left, but needed him to come that same day if he wanted one. It happened to be the day of the blizzard. He left work and drove a long distance to pick up our new girl. When he arrived, there were two puppies sitting in a baby's playpen. He didn't know which to choose, but after a very short while, he began to bond with Chelsea.

After he brought her home, my husband went back out into the storm to buy toys, bowls, food, and a kennel. When he got back, I placed Chelsea in the kennel on the floor near our bed, so she would know we were nearby. I used a flashlight to check on her throughout the night.

Three days later, Chelsea had her first exam and I loved the veterinarian and his staff. They were kind and did everything possible to ensure that our new girl felt comfortable in this initial visit. In the sixteen years Chelsea and I spent together, her health and well-being were my number one priority. She never missed her annual exams, treatments, shots, vitamins, or grooming. You could count on one hand the number of times we boarded her since I never wanted to travel anywhere that didn't allow dogs. On the rare occasions when she had to be kept at a kennel, I gave the staff three pages of instructions for her daily routine as well as her favorite blanket, treats, and toys.

Chelsea was very smart and quickly learned my routine, and my morning and evening rituals. As a professional nurse, my job was flexible enough to allow me to go home during the day and check on Chelsea. I had bought her a ball that had the capability to record my voice, so when she played with it, she could hear me saying how much I loved her.

Later in my career, I was able to work from home, so my bond with Chelsea grew even stronger. We loved watching television, playing with her toys, sleeping side-by-side, and eating popcorn together. Yes, that's right! Popcorn was Chelsea's special treat – she absolutely loved it. She also loved my husband, my children, and any guests who came to our home, welcoming them with her playful manner and adorable personality.

As a puppy Chelsea behaved like a little human and her veterinarian would regularly say, "Chelsea thinks she is one of us." We agreed since she preferred our company to that of other dogs. Throughout her lifetime, she would run and hide if another dog tried to be friendly. She never bonded with other animals, and would shake with fear at any kind of veterinary appointment, even if it was just a grooming.

As the years went by, I kept a closer watch on Chelsea's health. Sometimes this required more frequent veterinary visits, exams, and lab testing. I was determined to keep ahead of any potential changes. My training as a nurse came in handy because I was able to collect her stool and urine samples for each visit. When Chelsea was about thirteen years old, her lab results suggested she might have Cushing's Disease, a malady that arises when the endocrine system secretes too many hormones, especially cortisol, in the body. After consulting with her vet and doing my own research on the disease, I learned that Chelsea could live up to five more years with the disease.

She had, it turns out, nearly three more years of a very good life with us. Our vet believed it was the love and care we provided, along with her will to live, that allowed her to get through the next few years. As her sixteenth birthday approached, I noticed changes in Chelsea's behavior; undue panting, and an increased appetite and thirst. These were common symptoms of Cushing's Disease.

We returned to the vet and tests revealed Chelsea had an extremely high white blood cell count. We were asked to return for a follow-up visit in two months. Within that time frame, Chelsea's behavior began to change. She lost her appetite, and for the very first time, she started having accidents on the floor.

In December 2015, the vet suggested different diets and treatments. New lab work showed her kidney values had declined and that overall, she wasn't doing well. When I received these results, I immediately began to cry. I was told that Chelsea could begin fluid treatments three times a week, or if I wanted, I could take her to a specialist for an ultrasound to receive more feedback. Our vet knew her time was limited, but he was very compassionate. I asked him if she was in pain; he said it was difficult to tell. All I knew was that I didn't want Chelsea to suffer.

My husband and I decided to begin the fluid treatments and made an appointment for the ultrasound. I wanted to understand the extent of Chelsea's condition, in order to make the best decision. After the procedures, the specialist said that based on the findings, if Chelsea was his dog, he would euthanize her. When I heard that word, I began crying and wanted to leave. My husband asked for a more detailed explanation of her condition. The results were not good: The ultrasound revealed masses, and severe abnormalities within her kidneys. My husband also asked how much time he thought Chelsea had to live. The specialist said about one month.

We took Chelsea home, then returned to her primary veterinarian the next day, which was December 16, 2015. Our vet was very kind and said, "You don't have to make the decision this moment. You know Chelsea and she knows you, and the love is there. If you want to take her home with you, do that." I chose to take her home. That evening Chelsea did not eat and was very quiet. I held her and put her in a diaper, as she was unable to control her bladder. Then, Chelsea cried. It was the first time I had ever heard her cry. I knew it was time. I called our vet who said we could bring her to the office that evening, or his team would come to our home the next morning.

In my heart, I didn't want to let Chelsea go but I couldn't let her suffer either. After spending time in prayer, I decided that the following morning would be best. I called our children to explain my decision and they all agreed to be present when the doctor came. Later that night, I left Chelsea alone for ten minutes, so I could finish something in our home office. When I returned, she had begun her transition. I quickly picked her up and began sobbing uncontrollably. I told Chelsea how much I loved her, asked what I would do without her, and thanked her for sharing sixteen years with me. I was very confused and distressed because I didn't understand how her condition could have changed so quickly. That evening my little Chelsea passed away in my arms. I held her until my husband took her from me.

In the morning, we took Chelsea to our vet's office, where they arranged for her cremains. They also provided us with a clay imprint of her paw. Our vet was very helpful when he saw how difficult it was for me to cope with Chelsea's death. He recommended a pet loss support group called Beyond the Paw Print. I started attending the meetings two months after Chelsea passed away and continued to attend sessions every month for nearly two years. My connection with Dr. Micky was immediate, and I trusted that she truly cared about me and listened without judgment. Finding this group was a true blessing. I did not tell anyone about the sessions because family and friends often don't understand the love that exists between you and your pet. Beyond the Paw Print was there for me. I am so grateful to have found this organization.

I continue to treasure Chelsea's belongings – her toys, clothing, collar, leash — even her baby gate and medical records. It took me almost a year before I could eat popcorn again, since it was one of the snacks Chelsea and I enjoyed together. I still light a candle for her every single day. It's been my faith in God that has helped carry me through such a heartbreaking event.

I knew too that I needed to create something in Chelsea's memory, something I could see every day. Gardening is one of my greatest passions, and Chelsea and I spent many happy hours together in our yard. When springtime arrived, with those memories as my motivation, I created "Chelsea's Garden," named just that with a plaque I had specially made. It is the first thing I see when I walk into the yard and it makes me smile. Soon after, our family gathered for a remembrance service at our home where we released sixteen balloons in Chelsea's honor and planted a tree in her garden. At Christmas time, we still hang her stocking and ornaments, and display a treasured photo album of her life, created by our children.

One day, I will have the strength and courage to let go of all of her items. In time, I may even think about getting another puppy. With prayer and the support of Beyond the Paw Print, we will see. For now, I'm grateful that my prayers were answered, and that Chelsea received her angel wings on her own terms. I still harbor feelings of sadness and guilt for not being by her side while she was slipping away. I continue to ask myself, "Was she in any pain??" Some say that at their time of death, those who are leaving this world need to do so alone. Chelsea needed to leave on her own, quietly. Her death is still hard to accept, and I think of her in those final moments, more than anything.

In the three years since Chelsea's been gone, I have kept busy in a variety of ways. I find fulfillment through my family, my role as an RN (on a contingent basis), and am very active, along with my husband Calvin, at our church. Together we are co-leaders of the married couples' ministry. I'm also the director of our health and healing ministry, a member of the quilting and the Women of Hope ministries. Calvin volunteers on the ministerial staff and sings in the men's choir. We both find much comfort and meaning in these activities.

Life is a collection of moments, with many small, happy experiences that we need to savor and enjoy every day. I'm grateful that Chelsea was with us for sixteen long years, and that we were the recipient of her unconditional love. She will forever be my best friend and my little baby. I send hugs to all who are grieving. I now understand.

SABRINA

STORY SIXTEEN

I was Bewitched

By Kristine

MY CAT SITTER AMY THOUGHT OF ME immediately when she'd heard about a five-week old kitten found dirty and hungry on a busy four-lane street. Would I be willing to give her a home? At the time I had a sixteen-year old Calico named Samantha, who was being treated for renal failure, and had just lost my cat Tiffany two months earlier. I told Amy that in order to take the kitten I'd need to see how she interacted with Samantha before I made a commitment.

When the two were introduced, Samantha was instantly aloof. Despite her behavior, I was unable to resist the frightened furry baby in our midst. I fell in love with this beautiful, energetic, smart, green-eyed grey tabby, and decided to keep her. I named her Sabrina. I was bewitched.

Little Sabrina wanted Samantha to mother her, but Samantha ignored all of her efforts. Samantha was devoted to me and refused to bond with the kitten. For example, one evening Sabrina was sitting on one side of me and Samantha on the other. Sabrina came over to cuddle with Samantha, but Samantha wanted no part of it. She promptly got up and took her place on the other side of me. She simply did not want to be friends. During her lifetime, Samantha loved being near me; she was a true lap cat. When I had back surgery several years earlier, my mother had to care for both me and Samantha! Mom had to entertain her and allow Samantha to sleep on her lap in order to distract her from entering my room and sitting on my back, as she was used to.

It was only two years later that my vet told me Samantha didn't have much longer to live. Her kidneys were failing, and her little body was beginning to bloat. Despite various medical interventions, her health continued to deteriorate. A heart-wrenching decision needed to be made, as I watched and listened to Samantha pace the length of my bed, meowing throughout the night. I knew it was time to put Samantha out of her misery. I knew she was hurting. Saying goodbye was going to be incredibly difficult, I understood that all too well. Luckily, a kind friend accompanied us to the vet's office. I held my girl and told her how much I loved her. After our final goodbye, I felt like I'd lost a piece of my heart.

After Samantha's death, Sabrina took over lap duty. She was a bright, cute, and talkative kitty and I loved her dearly. Sabrina had more energy than any of my previous cats, delighting in games of catch wherein I'd throw her small balls which she'd then try to clasp between her tiny paws; she was great at it. If there was a cat basketball team, she'd be the star!

Sabrina was a little bit of a thing, barely seven pounds even when fully grown. I nicknamed her Breezy because she flew around like a breeze. She was skittish though, and was initially always afraid of strangers, until curiosity drew her out of her hiding place. I had a second-story deck that she loved, chasing dragonflies and jumping at bugs until she caught them. Everybody thought she was adorable.

When Sabrina was about two years old, a stray tuxedo cat appeared at our front door, meowing constantly, as if to say "Let me in." It was very cold, and I didn't think that she'd make it through the winter. I let the cat in but initially kept her separated from Sabrina. The cat, it turns out, had had a variety of health issues and had obviously been abandoned. About six months Sabrina's junior, I named her Moo since her black-and-white coloring resembled a cow.

Moo accepted Sabrina as the alpha cat, a respect level that remained intact for the ten years they lived together. Even though they weren't best friends, they got along well. Sabrina and I had a very close relationship. She always purred with contentment when around me and was happiest when on my lap or sleeping by my side. I truly loved this little green-eyed minx. Our bond was very strong.

As the years passed, life was good for my two girls. Since I didn't have children, I spoiled my cats with all of my love. I traveled frequently for my job as an auto executive, much to the chagrin of both of them. When my cat sitter moved out of state, I needed to find someone equally kind and conscientious. I was referred to a wonderful woman, Rita, who shared my passion for felines. Rita willingly took on her new role, but was not able to stay overnight since she had cats of her own at home. Her love of animals was evident, and she spoiled my two girls too, with my wholehearted approval. We became great friends, so much so that Rita helped me through the loss of both of my parents. Eventually I was able to retire, which gave me more time to enjoy life and my cats.

Three years ago, my sister Karen, who lives in Florida, became engaged and I flew down with my siblings for her wedding. As part of my travel routine, I left my kitties under Rita's care. The day after the wedding, while enjoying some beach time,

I received a phone call at 10:30 in the morning from my security company. They told me the fire alarm was going off at my house. The police were delayed in getting there though since another fire was happening at the same time in the area. The security company called a second time: I learned that my house was on fire. I phoned a few of my neighbors but got no answer. I put my hometown and the word "fire" into a search engine and found a picture of flames coming through my roof.

A call to the police confirmed my worst fears. I immediately called the airline and changed my ticket to return home that night. Rita was in church that morning and had silenced her phone, unable to receive my calls and texts. When she looked at her phone, she saw my messages and immediately drove to my home. She was devastated by the sight: My home had burned to the ground, and my next-door neighbor's home was also destroyed.

A brave fireman had entered my home and found both cats on my bed. Moo froze and the fireman was able to grab her, but Sabrina ran out of the room. With the fire and smoke all around them, the fireman had to move swiftly to get out of the house, taking Moo with him. He placed her in his car and a kind neighbor loaned Rita a carrier, so she was able to bring Moo to her home until I arrived later that night. Moo smelled of smoke but was otherwise okay.

My home looked like a bomb had gone off, with only a shell of the exterior left standing. I called for Sabrina in the nearby woods; but got no answer. I hoped and prayed that she was alive, but I realized that she may not have survived. The fire marshal said she could be alive since they had broken all the windows in the house. This is a standard practice that allows dangerous gasses to escape from a burning home.

Early the next day, after searching nearby areas, there was still no sign of Sabrina. The fire marshal however had made a different discovery. When he went into the house again, he discovered Sabrina's body, found in the screened-in porch of my lower level by the back door. This was one of her favorite places, so I wasn't surprised that she sought refuge there. It was the one window that had not been broken down during the fire; had it been, she might have escaped. When the fire marshal handed her to me, I was completely devastated. Holding her lifeless little body and imagining her final moments, was overwhelming. I was overcome with grief, nausea, and horror as I realized how she must have suffered. A kind neighbor and the fire marshal did their best to provide comfort. Together with my neighbor, we took Sabrina's body to be cremated, my final goodbye.

The loss of my Sabrina, and the way she died, was more distressing than everything else I had lost put together. I couldn't imagine life without her. Dealing with the insurance company and all the other details related to the fire kept me extremely busy during the day. The fire marshal discovered that it was the neighbor who had accidentally started the fire. This news caused additional distress and I cried my heart out every night and missed my little girl more than I can say.

My trauma was severe, and I was unable to process it alone. I knew I needed help with my grief. The minister from my church provided support, kindness, and reassurance as well as reading materials during that difficult time. I learned that the trauma I felt over the loss of Sabrina and my home were similar to that felt after other major losses. I needed time to heal, as well as more support, and I needed others with whom I could share my story.

I soon found what I was looking for: Beyond the Paw Print, an in-person support group, held monthly meetings for those suffering the loss of a pet. I phoned the number listed on the website and was able to speak to its founder, Micky. She willingly let me share the story of my loss and the overwhelming emotions that came with it. Micky encouraged me to attend a support group meeting, which I agreed was necessary. I like to bake and decided I'd bring brownies to the meeting, hoping they would bring a little bit of comfort to everyone in attendance. I must have been onto something as the plate was empty by the end of the meeting!

I attended several meetings, and discovered I wasn't alone in my grief. At the first meeting, I was a mess. I cried the entire time as I spoke about my loss, as did most of the other newer attendees. They understood the pain of my loss through their own. At one meeting, I was fairly shocked to learn that one of the attendees was a therapist. A mental health professional was at a meeting, seeking support, too! She spoke of her devastation over the death of her own pet. She said she could hardly get out of bed and took a week off from work. If a therapist could feel the same way I did, maybe I'm not as bad off as I thought.

Micky is a treasure and very wise. As a result of her own pet losses and the lack of support she experienced, she was motivated to create BTPP. At the meetings, Micky has many books and resources for grieving pet owners. Her love, wisdom, advice, and empathy are evident, and her desire to help grieving pet owners is completely selfless. She is able to support and soothe, ask relevant questions, and make helpful suggestions. She asks us to try to remember the joy and love we shared with our pets throughout their lives, not just the sadness at the end of life. The upshot for me: I felt better after each meeting and have been able to go on.

In the aftermath of the fire and Sabrina's death, I moved to a rented condo not far from where I had lived. The stress and aggravation of getting my former home demolished and rebuilt, and dealing with an unethical builder took its toll on both Moo and me. Moo spent a great deal of time in her carrier and wasn't acting normally. When I found blood in her urine, I took her to the vet. The vet discovered Moo had a urinary tract infection and bladder stones. Fortunately, she passed the stones and is healthy once again. The vet explained that human beings aren't the only ones who suffer from Post-Traumatic Stress Disorder (PTSD) and said that Moo exhibited signs of this too. Before the fire, she could have slept through a sonic boom; after the fire, any loud noises set Moo on edge. I can't imagine her being in the middle of that chaos, especially with the unfamiliar and frightening sounds of the sirens, windows crashing, alarms, and water hoses. How frightening it must have been. During the first dark weeks after the fire, Moo actually put her paw in my hand at night. Another time she hugged me on my upper arm with both paws. She has not offered this up since, but I'm just so grateful that she survived the fire. I am blessed to have this special animal by my side.

One day in our rental home, Moo's PTSD reached its height when maintenance workers were repairing the roof and siding. The noises from the ladders, the hammering, and loud voices triggered her fear. Moo hid under the bed and fortunately I was there and able to soothe and comfort her. Moo never hides — under the bed or anywhere — so I could tell she was truly scared. Two-and-a-half years later, I'm happy to report that she is much better. Her PTSD has abated, and she is in a healthy state.

Although it's unconventional and for some, controversial, I found help from the messages of a pet communicator, a person that can talk to your pets both on earth and in heaven. Through my session with a communicator, I felt reassured that I'd see my Sabrina again. I learned that she tried everything she could to keep breathing, to survive.

The pet communicator said that Sabrina often visits me and is present in the shadows I see out of the corner of my eye, or when I see footprints on a blanket that my Moo doesn't use — which I've seen. The communicator also said that Sabrina reported that while she was alive, there was an older woman who visited me regularly, someone whom I'm sure was my mother. Sabrina also said that this woman helped her to the other side when it was her time. My mother, so I have been told, has also imparted to Sabrina that she could come with her to greet me when it's my time to pass over.

Through the two years it took to get my home rebuilt, I realized that I wanted to live closer to my family. With two of my sisters in Florida, this was the perfect opportunity to make a move. Moo and I are now thriving in our new home in the Sunshine State. I miss not having two cats, but my girl would more than likely not welcome another cat at this time in her life. I hope to adopt two older cats after she's gone.

Saying I'm grateful doesn't even begin to describe what the BTPP meetings have done for me. The friendships that have developed through this group provided the comfort and consolation I so badly needed during an incredibly tragic time. I encourage grieving pet owners to attend a support group. Search the internet or ask your veterinary office for referrals for a group in a nearby community. It is cathartic to be with other grieving pet owners who feel as broken as I did.

Making donations to a few local animal shelters in Sabrina's memory has been another helpful channel to processing my grief. It's been my human family and Moo, who have become the rocks in my life, and we've all grown even closer as a result. They have been there 1,000 percent for me through this whole experience.

I still miss my little beauty. I talk to Sabrina all the time, and I will never forget the friendship, love, and joy she brought into my life. I have the ashes of three of my former cats, Tiffany,

Samantha, and Sabrina in a special place. When it's time for Moo to receive her angel wings, her ashes will join them, too. When I die, my cats' ashes will be mixed with mine, and we will all fertilize a garden and be together again. Till then, I am grateful for today and all the blessings that surround me and my family.

ANNIE

STORY SEVENTEEN

She was Meant for Me

By Shari

MY 40TH BIRTHDAY WAS APPROACHING and the only thing at the forefront of my mind, besides the milestone event, was rescuing a dog. As a single woman, I lived alone and decided a dog would make a wonderful companion. I had recently bought a house with a large yard, key to providing a good home for a canine. When I was a child, we had a Collie, a Lassie double, a beloved dog who had left me with many happy memories of the years we spent together. I wanted to experience that kind of happiness and unconditional love again.

My search began. Weeks turned into months as I visited multiple shelters hoping to meet that special someone. I almost gave up. Every dog I saw was inevitably compared to my beloved Collie, and each one came up short. None had touched my heart in that, "I'm yours, and you're mine" kind of way. My search continued.

As time passed, I began to think perhaps my latent maternal instincts just might be better left dormant … until I saw Duffy. I was walking through one of the local shelters filled with hopeful faces and saw the saddest pup, a beautiful yellow Labrador Retriever. Duffy kept her eyes cast down on the dreary grey cement floor, as if she felt unworthy of eye contact with a potential owner. Something in me stirred, and I knew it was meant to be. This forlorn, but sweet young dog and I would make each other happy. I just had to know the reason for those sweet yet heartbreaking eyes.

I soon learned that Duffy had lived a happy life in a busy household with three young children. Her family had made the decision to have her re-homed. With another child on the way, they sadly had neither the time nor the energy for this otherwise rambunctious and fun-loving dog.

The name Duffy was too generic for my liking, so I considered other options. One name instantly came to mind: Annie. The tale of Little Orphan Annie was about a girl without a family, and this dog had the same story. She had been put in an animal orphanage, and abandoned by her human mama, papa, and siblings. This was my Little Orphan Annie. This beautiful Lab would be an orphan no more. I would devote my life to making those eyes sparkle again, shining with joy and love.

As soon as we got home, Annie showed me just what an awesome dog she was. She caught on to her new name within two days, and quickly learned the ropes when it came to my house and yard. It was clear that she had a high level of intelligence, but she also appeared confused and unhappy. When she looked up at me with her big brown eyes, I could sense a sadness from deep within. Neither treats nor new toys seemed to lift her spirits for quite some time.

Her confusion soon became apparent: If a child was crying on TV, Annie would look alert, as if thinking, "There they are!" She would even go up to the television and paw at the screen, trying to touch the children. She would sit on the sofa in the living room and stare out the window for hours, as if waiting for her family to come and take her back home. It was easy to imagine what she was wondering: "Who is this person? And most of all, when will I return home to my family?" I hoped my love and affection would soon fill her heart.

After a while, Annie got used to her new life and happily, we became more than the best of buddies, we became soul mates. She understood my moods almost more than I did. She knew when I needed hugs, smiles, or sloppy kisses and knew when we needed a walk — to get exercise, fresh air or a fresh perspective, even when I wasn't feeling up to it — by giving me a doggy smile and a fiercely wagging tail, followed by prancing over to the door. Annie made the dreary cold winter months manageable with her lighthearted spirit. We were inseparable for the next twelve plus years.

The nature of my career was such that it required fairly frequent geographical change, so Annie and I moved a lot. We lived in Milwaukee, Chicago, Boston, and then Detroit. We took long hikes, regardless of weather or terrain. We befriended many — both human and canine — at Chicago's dog beaches on the shores of Lake Michigan, Harvard University's Arboretum, and the dog parks in Milwaukee. We then spent a very happy six years in Beverly Hills, Michigan, a suburb of Detroit, where we lived in a big house filled with sofas. She loved spending her lazy, aging days napping in the sunshine or keeping watch on the squirrel, chipmunk, and deer populations in our yard. Our neighborhood had many dogs of all types, ages, and personalities. Our daily strolls up and down the street felt like a continuous dog party, as everyone cheerily greeted and sniffed at each other, especially in the wintertime when there was an abundance of snow to romp in.

As the years went on, Annie's yellow fur faded to white, and her hips and bones gradually took to aging as well. She wanted shorter walks and didn't have the same zest for tug of war or for playing with her toys. Her appetite was decreasing — even for her treats. Her visits with the neighbor dogs were more like a quick hello than the joyous reunion they'd always been. I just knew that her time was approaching, albeit gradually. As I watched Annie deteriorate, I knew I had to prepare myself *and* not allow the grief to cripple me. But, how?

My prayers were answered when I saw a flyer about Beyond the Paw Print Pet Loss Support Group. I had never heard of a group that helped grieving pet parents and hoped this could help me when Annie would ultimately pass away. Annie was still alive but not 100 percent well, and I felt that I needed this group as a preventative measure. Just looking at my dog brought an onslaught of tears. The anticipation of her leaving me already produced physical pain. I felt like I was being punched in the stomach whenever I thought about it, my heart both racing and aching as a result. It was physically hard to breathe when I tried to imagine my life without my sweet soulmate.

I decided to attend my first BTPP meeting despite feeling silly and self-conscious that I, unlike other participants, was still blessed to have my dog with me. I hadn't yet experienced her death. Through the group, I learned that there is a name for this type of sorrow: anticipatory grief.

I was stunned when I saw Micky's wide array of literature on display at each meeting. There were books, pamphlets, and flyers – all related to pet loss. Prior to attending this meeting, I'd felt alone, dreading the grief that loomed on the horizon. With so much material on the subject, it was obvious there were many in need of guidance and support with their grief. This was enough to give me the boost of confidence needed to continue to attend meetings each month, despite Annie's still being around.

She was ailing, and I could feel the end quickly approaching. Annie's beautiful chocolate-colored eyes told me she was ready. Despite our unconditional and immeasurable love for each other, her wise, beautiful soul shone through, as if she were truly asking me to help her cross over. Yet I suffered with all of the unknowns; was it too soon, or not yet time? I agonized over the decision, one of the biggest of my life.

Eventually, Annie's physical state was enough to let me know when it was time to say goodbye. She went into sudden organ failure. Time was of the essence and I knew I needed to put an end to her excruciating pain. Fortunately, I had found a wonderful mobile veterinarian who was able to come to the house to put my girl to sleep. I am so grateful we'd been able to say goodbye in the comfort of our own home. Annie was surrounded by photos of everyone who loved her, like my parents, friends both human and canine; and those of the two of us over the years. Because Annie had always gravitated toward any room where music was being played, I ensured that soft music could be heard in the background. Candles were lit to cast a soft glow on the late winter afternoon sun. Annie was on her favorite soft bed, her eyes locked with mine as the veterinarian's first injection of medication helped her to fall asleep quickly, while the next injection caused her heart to stop beating.

I expected that I would be wailing, sobbing, unable to get myself up off the floor where I was holding her. But I was surprised with my inner strength. The next day I awoke, and instead of feeling incapacitated by my heartbreak, I felt resolute. I knew it was the right time for Annie's passing. It wasn't too soon, and it wasn't too late. It was peaceful and serene. Annie crossed the Rainbow Bridge and received her angel wings on February 11, 2013. I asked that her cremation be accelerated, and her ashes were returned to me just three days later. It was important for me to be reunited with Annie on Valentine's Day, since she had been the joy and love of my life. I'm so grateful that I had been proactive and taken one year to emotionally prepare for the loss of my girl. It made all the difference.

After Annie's death, I continued to attend the BTPP meetings. I found the meetings beneficial in a variety of ways. First, there was no pressure to talk. If talking about my loss elicited tears or my throat became too constricted to speak, it was OK to pass, and Micky would kindly move on to another attendee. I never felt embarrassed.

Second, I also enjoyed the fact that we were encouraged to bring photos of our beloved pets. I wasn't the only one who often walked in clutching my pet's photo tightly to my chest. It provided a sort of tangible strength during each meeting and helped us put a face on our pets when speaking about our loss and our journey through grief. I was so proud of Annie. I loved sharing photos which captured her beauty, while I described her wonderful qualities.

I will always be indebted to the open hearts, minds, and generous spirits of my fellow meeting attendees, and I've learned so much from each of them. Most of all, I've benefited from Micky's caring spirit. She gently supported me through my grief, which not only helped me function, but also to recognize that I could be proud of the love I had for my dog, rather than to hide my feelings. Attending this kind of support group helped me see that I wasn't alone, nor crazy. I discovered that my grief was legitimate, and that I no longer had to grieve in isolation. The meetings created a space where each of us could freely express our feelings of love and loss. We could confront a range of emotions in a safe, confidential space.

If I were to give any advice to someone grieving the loss of a pet, I would say that you have the right to do so, in your own way. Your journey is unique. No two people will experience this loss in the same way, so never compare your situation or reactions to anyone else's. Be gentle with yourself and never be ashamed of your grief. Allow yourself to fully experience your sorrow — as long as necessary. Some have said that grief over the loss of a pet is harder than that for a human. We share an unconditional love with animals, often not the case when it comes to our human relationships, which can be fraught with unpleasant baggage. Those who react to an outward expression of grief with, "It's just a dog!" or "It's just a cat!" should be ignored. They've obviously never known the beautiful, blessed connection between humans and their pets.

I allowed myself almost two full years to grieve, rather than to rescue a new dog right away. At that point, I felt I had worked through the losses of both my childhood dog and my beloved Annie. No dog could replace Annie, I knew that, but no dog needed to. I was ready to love again. My heart was big enough, and I felt a renewed desire to adopt a new dog to care for, love, and protect.

The next love of my life is quite a character — actually the opposite of Annie. Since I feared I might make an unfair comparison, I sought out someone who was different in every way. Instead of a girl, I got a boy. Instead of a large dog, I adopted a small one. Instead of a purebred, I took in a mutt. My new little guy, Brody, is — ready for this? Brody is a Beagle/Corgi/Chihuahua mix, who arrived spoiled rotten on the day I brought him home. My little guy is small but has a big personality, and a strong sense of importance. He makes me laugh every day, and I love the new challenge of getting to know and work through his eccentricities. I knew almost right away that rescuing Brody and loving a new dog didn't mean I was betraying Annie or, most of all, replacing her, because she was irreplaceable. Love is infinite.

I still honor Annie and her memory with an altar that I placed atop my fireplace mantel. It's where I keep her paw print that the veterinarian had made before she passed away, and several photos of the two of us together. I also keep a candle with Annie's name on it from a BTPP group memorial service led by Micky, and I have her ashes with me in a beautiful urn, which helps keep her close to me as well. Sadness and tears are now a thing of the past, giving way to smiles and chuckles about the happy times that I'll remember forever.

SULLY

He was a Gift I Couldn't Refuse

By Brady

IT WAS 2004 AND ONLY TWO YEARS SINCE I had said goodbye to my last best friend, Shelty, a Corgi/Sheltie mix. The pain from losing my dog was so great that I vowed I would never get another one, ever. My daughter felt differently. Rachel had launched into a search — without telling me — for a purebred male Sheltie. When she found a breeder in Indiana who had puppies born on May 9th, she knew this was a sign from God: May 9th just happens to be my birthday. Three weeks later, we found ourselves in the car driving to the shelter to claim one of the dogs for our own. I was reluctant at first, unsure if I was ready. When we got to the farm and the breeder handed over the seven-week-old puppy we had chosen, my heart melted. I began to cry. I knew that this dog would be my new best friend.

But what to call this handsome pup? My wife Cheryl and I brainstormed along with our three children, but nothing sounded right. My son Jeremy finally suggested we call him Sully, since we were avid fans of the *Dr. Quinn Medicine Woman* series, and one of the main characters in the series had that name. Sully it was.

What I enjoyed most about Sully was just being with him; as long as he and I were together, we were completely content. Our walks were the best part of the day, usually taken to his favorite spot, a wooded area with several miles of walking trails. Sully loved to herd birds too, especially seagulls at the beach. I also convinced him that jet planes were really big birds. To his last day, he would bark at every plane that flew overhead and try to herd it.

After thirteen wonderful years with my boy, Sully started to suffer from three significant maladies common in older dogs. He developed difficulty in swallowing, an inflammation of the pancreas, and kidney failure. I knew the inevitable was coming but just didn't know when. Over the next three months, I hoped and prayed that Sully's health would improve, but instead it continued to decline. As walking became a struggle, especially through our favorite stretch of the woods, I would pull Sully in a wagon. He did his best to enjoy it, but I could see when he began to grow weary.

One thing I could do for Sully was give him fluid by injection under the skin every day to sustain his hydration, which was suffering as a result of his kidney failure. Our vet instructed me on how to administer the fluids, and it became part of our daily routine. I prayed that God would take Sully peacefully so I wouldn't have to make the choice to let him go. The guilt and uncertainty over having to euthanize my dog was more than I could take. It would be so much easier if God would just step in, but that was not to be His will. God seemed to be telling me that loving also meant letting go.

April 2, 2018 was our last day together. I gave Sully his breakfast and took him for his last walk in the woods in the wagon. We stopped and sat under a tree on a blanket for several hours. As we left the woods, I knew we would never return, and I wept uncontrollably. It was 2:00 in the afternoon when we got home, and the hospice vet was scheduled to arrive at 3:00. Jeremy came over and brought Sully a small pizza. It was his favorite treat. He ate as much as he could and drank some water. The vet had arrived by this time and Sully and I were sitting on our favorite spot on the back deck. I wrote the following letter to him, which explains the rest of what happened that day.

My Dear Sweet Sully,
You were born on May 9, 2004, and just seven weeks later you came into my life. Neither one of us knew what the future would hold but for me, it was love at first sight.
As I watch the slide show I made to remember you, I'm overwhelmed. You were part of everything I did, and I never wanted to be away from you for even one night.
We had nearly fourteen years together (in dog years, you were 84!), but it seems like such a short amount of time.
That fateful day when you left this earth made me realize that everything worth having comes at a price. I want to thank you for your strength throughout the whole ordeal.
Thank you for the way you helped me do what had to be done. I believe our spiritual and emotional connection transcended most human relationships.
Before I had to let you go, we were sitting on the deck in our favorite spot and you were gazing into the backyard, scanning it from left to right as if you knew it would be your last time. That's when I told you what was about to happen, that you were going to be set free from all of your pain, that you would be going to heaven to your True Master, and that you'd be made new again. You would be running and playing, barking and howling, and would once again be with all of the friends we had already lost. I knew you could understand every word I said. I couldn't always understand what you were feeling so when I told you how difficult this was for me, I asked for some way you could convey that I had your permission. The whole time I was talking, you were listening intently, your eyes never leaving mine. As I finished, I was weeping, and the tears were gushing down

my face. Although you had been very sick and refrained from giving me any affection when I asked for it, you immediately began to give kisses and lick away my tears as if to say, "I understand, it's OK. I just want to end this suffering and go to heaven. Don't be sad. I will run to you when you get there and we'll be together, never to be separated again." Thank you Sully, for helping me to let you go.

As you slowly slipped away, I only wish I could have known what you experienced. I never stopped kissing your face and speaking into your ear; telling you that I loved you and that I will never forget you. In just a few short moments, the vet announced that you had your angel wings. It was then that it hit, full force: You were physically gone and all that remained was your beautiful body and all the wonderful memories. We buried you right outside the window where I could see your resting place every day. We will make it a beautiful memorial garden where your memory will live on. You taught me so much about God's love and the meaning of life. I will grieve, but I promise you that your purpose, which has been perfectly fulfilled, will not be in vain. I'll go on, take what you taught me and apply it to everything I do for the rest of my life. I know God said to you when you arrived, "Well done thou good and faithful servant. Come witness the joy of the Lord." I will see you soon my beautiful brown-eyed baby boy. I love you Sully!

Your Loving Master,
Brady

After I lost my sweet Sully, I prayed for some kind of sign from God that he was OK and that I would see him again. Six days later, my younger daughter, Rebekah, was inspired to write a letter from Sully. She said that the words flowed through her, as if the Holy Spirit was guiding her hands. Here is what Sully had to say:

> Dear Master,
> I know how sad you are, and although I no longer feel emotions, I remember that my job on earth was to be your companion and to make you happy, so that's what I'll try to do. If you could only see what I have seen since I left you on that sunny day, you would be overjoyed. While on earth, you'll never be able to fully experience what it's like where I am, but since we are such kindred spirits, I think if I tell you about the wonderful adventure you sent me on, you'll have a better understanding of where I am.
> The last thing I remember is your voice telling me you loved me, and that you were going to help. I always knew that when you said, "I help," that meant we were going to do something together, and that I couldn't do it without you. It helped me relax, knowing that wherever we went, you were going with me. I remember feeling your kisses and your tears, and then the nice doctor was petting me, and things started to get warm and a little fuzzy. I began to feel like I was floating away, and for a moment I was scared because I saw that I was starting to float further from you and that you weren't coming with me, but I wasn't afraid for long. Soon, there was a warmth that spread through my entire body. It almost felt like I was lying in the sun at the beach in Oscoda, only better.
> I could still see you lying with me, I saw mommy crying, I

saw all my toys and could still hear the soft music playing in the background.

I could also see our house and our yard, and the route we walked every day. Even though I was getting further away, somehow, I could still see you clearly. You were crying, but for the first time in my life, your tears didn't make me sad. I understood why, and all I wanted to do was comfort you. Right at that moment though, a new instinct, stronger than anything I've ever felt before, drew me further and further from you and toward a beautiful, bright light, a light that was the source of the warmth I was feeling. For a moment I hesitated between looking down at you and looking at the light, but then I heard a voice coming from the distance that was gently calling — almost singing — my name:

"*Sully.*"

My ears perked up as the voice called again, louder and more glorious. My tail began to wag curiously.

"*Sully!*"

My heart started to pound with excitement as I realized that I *knew* this voice. I frantically sniffed the air to try to pick up a scent, but the smells were nothing like anything I had ever encountered, yet somehow, all familiar. The voice was getting closer, louder, and more fervent. The light was getting so bright I didn't think I could bear looking at it much longer. Just then, the light exploded into every possible color, and then the colors burst into even *more* colors and the brilliant rays surrounded me, forming a glorious sparkling rainbow. Everywhere I looked, the rainbow was there, arching over my head and wrapping under my paws. It was then, as I looked down, that I realized I was no longer floating, I was running, faster than I ever knew I could. I sensed that I was very near to the voice and could hear other voices joining it. They were singing something so beautiful, and ancient, and familiar, a melody that I had never heard but still, it resonated so much so that it almost felt like I had come from that music. The voice thundered so loudly I could feel the joy bursting from my chest.

"*SULLY!!*"

We were all singing and moving together, higher and further until we reached a shining white gate that flew open. The rainbow beneath me was glittering so intensely it looked alive. It then transformed into pure gold as it wound through the shimmering gate. The rainbow twisted over hills and valleys like a sparkling ribbon across a lush, gorgeous land, one I knew as well as our own woods, but had never been to before. Then I saw Him. Even the golden streets were dull compared to the brilliance of His face. I ran to Him and leaped into his arms as he gently laughed. He buried his face in my mane like you always did and whispered into my ear, "Well done, dear Sully. You served your master on earth faithfully, and you have pleased me. Welcome to your *true* home." I then followed him over a hill where a vast expanse of beach with no end stretched into the horizon. Hundreds of white birds flew in graceful flocks along the shoreline. I looked excitedly up at Him, asking permission. He smiled and bent down to hold my head in his strong hands.

"Go ahead, Sully. The birds don't mind. That's part of their job here and they too have been waiting for you to arrive." I kissed His kind face before I ran with more speed than the wind toward the flock of soaring birds, barking happily as I chased them back and forth along the crystal shore. Master, these are only the beginnings of my first moments of this adventure. You will have to wait to see for yourself. You won't understand it, even if I try to explain it to you, but I hope that this is enough to let you know what is ahead. Frankie and Elliot are here and whole again, with no pain or fear. Shelty, Sheba, and Barney all ran to greet me. We share happy memories about our life with you. You were the *best* and I love you so much. It's okay to feel sad and to cry, but I want you to know that sending me on this adventure was the kindest, most wonderful thing you have ever done for me. One day, you will see. I will be here, after you cross your own bridge and enter through the shimmering gate. I will be barking, right by His side, waiting to share this eternity with you.

All My Love,
Sully

This letter has given me hope and helped me through the grieving process. We must grieve; it's a part of healing. I once heard someone say that "grief is love trapped inside a heart with no place to go." What a perfect description.

I have fulfilled my promise to Sully, to create a memorial garden right outside our window, trying to pattern it after the beauty of the place he described in his letter to me. My grief however, continued to weigh so heavily on my heart. Rebekah was witness to this and suggested I attend a support group. She found Beyond the Paw Print Pet Loss Support Group online, and I reached out to Micky, the group's founder, right away. I attended the very next meeting.

Right from the beginning, I felt like I belonged and was able to share my story in a nonjudgmental, supportive, and comfortable environment. I openly grieved with the other attendees, each of whom were going through the same exact thing. When I noticed that other male attendees shed tears as they spoke of their loss, I was reassured that real men do cry!

I brought my daughter Rebekah to my second BTPP meeting and when it was my turn to speak, Micky gently invited Rebekah to share her inspirational letter from Sully to me and what had led her to write it. My daughter read the letter aloud and many found comfort in its words.

Although I continue to grieve, I get better each day. In addition to the group, I'm blessed with a very supportive wife and family who understand what I'm going through. They too are grieving and together we support one another. Through this difficult and painful experience, I've learned that there is hope. Instead of saying goodbye to Sully on that last day, I said I love you, I will always remember you and, most importantly, I will see you soon.

This is the hope that helps me face each new day. If I have a lasting mission as a result of this loss, it would be to share this story so others can find healing and hope. My prayer is that all who read this tribute will find comfort, too.

It has now been over one year since I lost Sully. After attending several BTPP meetings, I can honestly say that I have found an integral part of what I needed: support, acknowledgment, and validation that my grief was real, accepted, and understood. The resources Micky provides along with my own search for inspirational and supportive books has led me deeper in my faith and awakened within me an ultimate hope that can only be defined as the confident expectation and anticipation that something very good is coming. I celebrate the time I had with Sully, I celebrate life, and I know beyond the shadow of a doubt that I will see him again.

SABRINA & DAPHNE

STORY NINEEEN

Our Little Band of Three

By Marlene

I DON'T REMEMBER WHY I THOUGHT bringing a kitten home was a good idea, but at the age of 24, I must have wanted someone special to call my own. I had been renting the basement at my sister's house, and my job – in logistics for the auto industry — kept me very busy. I was often away from home as my role required frequent business trips to Mexico. In retrospect, I don't know that I considered the responsibilities entailed in the adoption of a kitten. My sister was the single mom of a six-year-old boy and already had two cats, Snowy and Michele. She had enough on her hands.

One Sunday afternoon, my friend Dana invited me to see a litter of kittens born in her parents' barn. Dana helped me pick out a kitty with just the right temperament. A kitty who agreed to be picked up, but also with an independent streak. Then she shared something surprising: "The one you're holding is a girl, because she's a Calico." During our visit, I held three different kittens and experienced three different reactions. One was too feisty, another too clingy, and the third was just right. She was a purring machine, and very loving but also slightly independent. She would be the one I would take home.

Since I didn't have a carrier, Dana gave me a basket with a lid, for the ride home. The kitten remained in the basket without ever attempting to escape. At one point along the way, I opened the basket and said to her, "Oh, you are a pretty one!" When we got to the house, my sister's cats welcomed her immediately. Michele started grooming her right away and Snowy just didn't seem to mind her at all. She belonged. I decided to name her Sabrina.

Determined to be a good mom, I promptly took Sabrina for her first vet visit. During the exam, she pulled loose from the vet's hands and jumped right into my arms. "Mom save me!" the vet joked. In that moment, I realized we were hopelessly in love with each other. I truly had become Sabrina's mom. I later learned she was a muted Calico with warm shades of gray and ginger, the latter color making a streak down her forehead and on the tip of her tail. Sabrina's eyes were so remarkably outlined too that she looked like she was wearing eyeliner, which contrasted beautifully with the many shades in her coat.

After about a year together, I found that my business travel was letting up. Happily, I was also in a place to finally move into my own apartment. Sabrina missed Snowy and Michele though and truly needed companionship. In order to get my attention, she would often swat at me. I quickly realized she needed kitty companionship. I had learned recently of a woman at work who rescued orphaned kittens so went to see the liter. All of them were black and white, except one. "I'll take the tabby," I said. The woman told me that this particular kitten had already been spoken for. Since none of the others felt quite right, I didn't take anyone else home that day.

Later in the week, the same coworker told me how she wished I would reconsider. She said she had put an ad in the newspaper, which had prompted several inquiries, even an unusual call from a woman who stated she wanted a kitten yet hadn't asked any questions or expressed any preferences. My coworker became suspicious because most callers at least ask about the kitties' appearance, age and background. She had recently learned that some people use kittens as snake bait. I certainly couldn't have it on my conscience that someone adopted kittens for that reason!

I told her that I'd adopt the kitty with the white tummy. A few days later, on Halloween 1998, the kitten I called Daphne joined our home. While initially Sabrina swatted at her new housemate, within a week they were nonstop playmates, and within three months, they were inseparable.

Sabrina and Daphne were with me through four moves, several relationships, and multiple career changes. "We're family," I'd always tell them. They seemed really happy in our little band of three, and so was I. They were a constant in my busy life as a single, career woman, and they had lovingly bonded with each other, which was so wonderful to see.

We spent fourteen wonderful years together, until 2012, when I was met with upsetting news. During a regular vet visit, Sabrina was diagnosed with kidney failure. I was devastated. Following the vet's instructions to the letter was my number one priority. Thankfully, our regular office visits revealed that she was doing okay. I told my girl that I hoped she would be with me all year, as I needed her and wasn't ready for my family to be disrupted by her death. Sabrina seemed to understand, and we had a good year together.

The following year started out rocky: This time it was me who had an emergency room visit. My boss was incredibly difficult, leading to heightened stress levels, which then resulted in severe gastric problems. I firmly believed Sabrina could sense my stress. One Sunday, she laid on my chest for at least an hour. This was very uncharacteristic. She was the cat who spent ten minutes with you and then went on her way. The next day, I shared this experience with a friend who responded, "She knows her mom needs her."

Soon after, my health issues improved but Sabrina's did not. One evening when I arrived home from work, I just knew something wasn't right. Sabrina appeared wobbly and ate very little. I called my sister in a panic. "There's only one Sabrina," my sister said. "Go to the vet now." I took Sabrina to the emergency animal hospital, where I hoped to learn that I had overreacted, and that all would be well. Within minutes, the vet gave me the news:

Sabrina was in a kidney crisis. He said she might improve, but needed to remain at the hospital so they could keep her hydrated.

I couldn't sleep and called him almost every hour. I knew my baby was terrified. Sabrina was released the next day after being on fluids for 24 hours. The vet taught me how to administer the fluids in order to keep her hydrated, but the next few weeks produced a sequence of incredibly painful events. The benefits of the treatment were only temporary, and her body was unable to tolerate the intervention. I tried to save her, but ultimately Sabrina was exhausted, and painfully, I opted to let her go. Throughout her life, Sabrina purred constantly, as if just being with me made her happy. With her very last breath, while in my arms, Sabrina continued to purr. I will always remember that moment.

Sabrina's passing hit me harder than I ever imagined it would. I sobbed and grieved for her with a depth unlike any loss I've ever felt. Sabrina was the type of cat everyone loved. People cried along with me, sent cards and flowers. Daphne was painfully anxious without her sister, and she was very clingy when I got home from work every day. I didn't know how to comfort her, beyond giving her all of my attention and love. I don't know if it helped Daphne; all I knew was that her presence was of great comfort to me.

When I reflect on her final moments, I felt like I let Sabrina down. I had placed her in the hands of an unfamiliar veterinarian who didn't seem to care about her. My little girl passed away under the care of someone who appeared nonchalant, with a business as usual demeanor. I'll always remember the vet's blank face — devoid of emotion — and his lack of compassion as I sobbed at the loss of my sweet kitty.

After Sabrina's death, I had dreams of rescuing sick cats. In reality, it was my cat I wanted to rescue. I was completely lost. After a few months of unrelenting grief and guilt, I decided to seek help. Through an internet search, I found Beyond the Paw Print Pet Loss Support Group and reached out to its founder, Micky, to learn more. It didn't take long for me to decide to attend the next meeting and share Sabrina's story. People listened and sympathized. I felt like I wasn't alone. I still hurt, but my grief has lightened because I had been *heard* by others who understood. They shared their losses as well, and how they were blindsided by the death of their pet. Like me, they too felt lost and were searching for answers.

As a result of the meetings, I was able to move forward and focus on loving Daphne. She needed me and she needed a fresh start with a new veterinarian who genuinely cared about her. I found a wonderful holistic doctor who not only helped me find the most appropriate food — just for her — but took the time to understand Daphne's needs as a senior kitty.

However, just three months after Sabrina passed away, Daphne stopped eating. At first, I thought she was being picky. Tastier food did the trick for a couple weeks, but then she stopped eating once again. I took her to the vet, hoping she'd discover the problem and make her well. The vet could not understand why her blood values were abnormal. I was referred to a specialist who performed an abdominal ultrasound on Daphne. The specialist was very optimistic. He said that given her age, he was surprised at how good things looked on the scan — she was perfect! The specialist said she had an infection and sometimes these things couldn't be named, but since she was improving and had excellent test results, I just needed to repeat the blood work with my normal vet in a week. In fact, Daphne had been given antibiotics, which were helping her feel better. Repeat blood work showed improvement, too. My girl returned to normal — for a week.

When she stopped eating again a few days later, my new vet ran the blood work once more. She called the very next day — normally her day off — and told me she wanted to run additional tests with the blood sample. Daphne's condition had deteriorated so severely that I took her to an emergency veterinary hospital recommended by my vet, and the same place where our specialist practiced. They admitted her and gave her fluids. They told me to take her home and wait for the test results.

Three days and one specialized test later, the vet called. Daphne had plasma cell myeloma, a type of cancer. They told me to bring her in and treatment could begin that same day. Thankfully, she went right into remission. What followed were six beautiful months together. Daphne was as normal and healthy as ever.

Ultimately, though, the treatments stopped working. I knew my girl truly couldn't hang on any longer. I also knew that we were not going to say goodbye at an animal hospital. I called the vet and arranged for an at home euthanasia, where Daphne could pass in familiar surroundings, in the bed she loved. Unlike with Sabrina, I had no regrets. She passed away thirty minutes before the vet arrived, in the place she knew, with just me by her side showering her with love. This is what she wanted — to end life on her own terms.

I reached out to Micky and attended a BTPP meeting, just three days after Daphne passed away. Like the previous meetings, I was heard, understood, and able to cry with the other attendees. My heart hurt from two losses in one year, but I felt more at peace and to this day, I look back and know that I did right by Daphne.

My special babies are together again. I can talk about them now with fondness rather than regret. Sharing experiences with those in the group helped me to feel whole and validated. Even after I stopped attending the group, I remained connected with some of the other attendees, and they supported me whenever I needed to share my grief.

I'm so grateful that I adopted a friend for Sabrina. However, Daphne was more than a companion cat. I came to know and appreciate her loving character, and her unique, beautiful soul. Sometimes when I remember my girls, I become teary, but now I recognize the love they brought me. I am grateful for the happy times we spent together. Their love helped me mature into adulthood. In fact, it was through Sabrina and Daphne that I learned how to give and receive love. They were my family. I believe they are now together again, touching paws in heaven.

Through both end-of-life experiences, I did encounter a few veterinarians who, despite their medical competency, lacked compassion for me as a pet parent. What I went through was traumatizing. It's important to have providers who care about both the patient and their guardian. Although I never complained about some of the less-than-ideal encounters, I continue to reflect on how much better the experience could have been if the doctors had been kind and compassionate, rather than detached and businesslike in their approach.

After Daphne died, I donated her food and litter to a local shelter. I held onto Daphne and Sabrina's toys though, since I suspected that I would adopt again, sooner rather than later. Within a month, I started looking for kitties available for adoption. I visited a shelter near my sister Cathy's home and spotted a kitty who looked like Sabrina and Daphne in one. She had a black and white mask-like face similar to Daphne's and an orange tail, similar to Sabrina's. I had to meet her! When the volunteer took her out of the cage, she jumped right into my lap. That said it all. We were meant for each other! I brought Olive home the next morning.

Then something very significant happened. I noticed that Olive's behavior patterns were very similar to Daphne's. She navigated her way around the house and laid on my chest in exactly the same way Daphne did. When I took Olive for her first check-up, my vet exclaimed, "Her spirit is just like Daphne's!" That reaction reinforced my belief that Olive and I were meant to be together. I told my vet that I was drawn to this cat by her colors, which reminded me of both of my girls. Adopting Olive has truly helped me to heal.

A neighbor recently showed me a photo she had taken of Sabrina and I felt overwhelmed with grief. Through my journey, I have discovered that we must accept this process; it's inescapable if we want to have animals in our lives. As I reflect on my life and the cats I have loved, I realize that the most important lesson Sabrina taught me is that I was lovable. She never wavered in her devotion to me and I truly considered myself her mom. There was no agenda, no judgment, just pure love.

AUSTIN

STORY TWENTY

Stone Cold Love

By Ellen

AUSTIN WAS THE SWEETEST DOG EVER. I know every owner says this, but to every owner, it's the truth. He came into our lives just as I was starting my career as a veterinarian in 2001. I learned pretty quickly that if my husband named our pets there was a greater likelihood of their gaining entrance into our family. My husband had been a big wrestling fan at the time, so he named our dog Austin in honor of the famous wrestler Stone Cold Steve Austin. We fell instantly for our new, young, Golden Retriever.

After a few years we decided to start a family. Little did I know that the years of trying to do so would produce a steady amount of infertility and loss. Austin was my loyal companion throughout, my stalwart support. When I finally became pregnant, Austin snuggled with me while I was on bed rest struggling to hold on to the baby we eventually lost. He was there to lick my tears, as both consoler and best friend. It took time, but our family, at long last, happened. We adopted Cordelia, our first child, in 2008 when she was six weeks old; eighteen months later, I gave birth to our second daughter, Lorelei. While not a fan of crying babies, Austin came to love both our girls, letting them crawl all over him as babies often do. His patience was boundless.

When Austin was eleven, I saw signs of something odd settling in. He started to wander out of the yard, which wasn't typical for him. Austin was always the kind of dog who ventured out, but would return to the door obediently, waiting to be let in; we never had or needed a fence. Twice, he wandered away, sending us to search the neighborhood for him. Luckily, our neighbors found him, our worst fears were never realized.

I thought at first this behavior could be old age or early dementia of some kind, since it lasted for many months. Austin also developed a slight cough, although it wasn't uncommon for him to cough after drinking too much water or while pulling on his leash during our walks. One night, I watched helplessly as Austin had what appeared to be a seizure. He lost control of his hind legs and collapsed on the floor. My years of emergency room experience instantly dissolved into the mist. I sat crying on the floor with my husband, trying to support Austin in his attempts to walk. Through our tears and distress, we discussed what should be done and how we would tell our girls. To our amazement, a few moments later *Austin recovered completely*. He walked over to me as if nothing had happened.

The following morning, I brought Austin to work in order to run some tests and consult with my colleagues. Radiographs of his chest revealed the cause of the seizures was cancer, which had originated in his brain, and had spread to his lungs. I was devastated.

My dog, by default, became my first hospice patient and teacher. After eleven years as an emergency room and critical care veterinarian, I was increasingly drawn to the emerging field of veterinary hospice and palliative care. We started Austin on steroids, anticonvulsants, and medication for pain. His response was remarkable! Much to my delight, he didn't have another seizure during the next four months. We got to celebrate one more Christmas with him. Every extra day was a blessing.

Unfortunately, everything changed in the new year. In early January, on his last day, Austin came in from his morning constitutional with his rear end covered in diarrhea. He had lost about ten pounds over the previous weeks and his appetite had been spotty. I had experimented with canned food to find something he liked; diarrhea was the unfortunate consequence. As I tried to hurry him into the shower to clean him off, Austin turned and snapped at me. My sweet boy had never shown one bit of aggression in his entire life. I sank to the floor and sobbed. It may have been due to the tumor in his brain. Maybe he was just tired of feeling sick. Whatever it was, I knew the decision I had to make.

My girls were three and four years old at the time. Since they were so young, I knew they wouldn't fully understand the concept of euthanasia. I gently explained that Austin was very sick and that we were going to help him die peacefully. We spent the day with him playing in the snow, one of his favorite things to do. They understood it as best they could.

That evening, my husband and I took Austin to the ER where I worked. My colleagues were wonderful. They dug through their dinners to find snacks to spoil him. We sat on the floor with Austin and snuggled close, for what felt like hours, soaking in every last touch and smell. While his passing was peaceful, his loss, for us, was excruciating. As a veterinarian, I'm supposed to be able to "fix" sick pets, yet I couldn't do this for my own. It felt like my worst failure. For most of my career, he'd gone to work with me, staying under my desk watching the chaos of those rushing into the emergency room with their urgent cases. This time, Austin wasn't coming home with me. The car felt so empty without him.

I was lucky that I had a few days off after Austin crossed the rainbow bridge. The clothes that I wore when we took him in that last evening smelled like him, a distinctive perfume of Fritos, which I now know is due to a particular bacterial flora on the skin of some dogs. I wore the same clothes for three days because it felt like the only way to stay close to him. When I did finally change, that outfit sat in the laundry bin for over a month. I didn't want to wash that smell away. I was clinging to every last physical memory that I could.

My lovely husband created a photo slideshow of Austin, set to some of my favorite songs. My girls and I would sit for long stretches of time, watching his pictures stream by, and I would tell them Austin stories from before they were born. It was healing for all of us.

After Austin died, I attended my first veterinary hospice conference with the International Association of Animal Hospice and Palliative Care (IAAHPC). I learned through Austin that palliative care makes a significant difference in a pet's end-of-life journey. Additionally, I learned that supportive preparation is essential for the family. When I left that conference, I was determined to start my own hospice practice. I discovered that I could transform my traumatic losses into something positive, and that changed the direction of my career.

After sixteen years in the ER, I launched Crossroads Veterinary Hospice. My training with the IAAHPC helped me to achieve my Certified Hospice and Palliative Care Veterinarian certification, or CHPV. In October 2017, I became one of the first vets in the world to specialize in hospice and palliative care, graduating with a class of around 60 candidates who completed the whole program. In addition to end-of-life issues, my practice includes treating senior pets for ailments such as arthritis and cognitive dysfunction. Transitioning from the ER to hospice required a significant amount of mental gymnastics. As veterinarians, we're taught to heal, with the goal of saving lives. Hospice care requires a different focus. I'm no longer trying to preserve life at all costs. Instead, my objective is to preserve quality of life, until it's no longer possible. In addition, I work closely with the family providing education and support during this very critical time.

My pet loss families are made aware that support is available after the passing of their pet. Beyond the Paw Print Pet Loss Support Group meetings allow owners to process grief and work toward healing in a nonjudgmental, supportive atmosphere. A few years ago, I contacted BTPP and asked Micky if she would allow me to sit in on one of her sessions. I explained that I wanted to learn ways I could better support grieving families. A date was set and a few months later, I found myself at a meeting – sitting in a semicircle among several new and returning attendees. My goal was to listen and learn. I never expected to share my story of Austin. As the evening drew to a close, Micky, who founded and facilitates BTPP, asked if I might like to speak about my work.

Surprisingly, I shared my story and found myself sobbing. It was about four years after Austin's death, yet there I was, crying uncontrollably. The group listened and supported me, as they had each attendee. I hadn't realized these feelings were so close to the surface and I was relieved to be able to process them in this supportive setting.

I learned firsthand the power of a pet loss support group. Since then, I've encouraged my clients to seek the help of BTPP. If group meetings are not for them, I recommend other forms of support, such as individual grief counseling, online support groups, or phone counseling with a local veterinary teaching hospital. I share this information with my grieving families so they will discover they are not alone, and that help is available. My journey with Austin led me to grief, then healing, and ultimately toward helping others as they struggled in similar situations. Thank you, Austin, my teacher, my consoler, my friend.

SCOUT

STORY TWENTY ONE

Unfulfilled Potential

By Karen

On an early spring day in 2012, I drove with my sister Lisa and her dog Lucky to a breeder I had found online. I would soon learn how much truth a simple search on the Internet can hide. Lisa and I observed the four pups he had available and picked the biggest and darkest one. We purposefully tried to match the color of our original family dog who was a Golden Retriever named Ranger. Because Dad and I loved military history and the great outdoors, we stuck to the same theme by calling our new puppy Scout. A stocky dog, I almost dropped him the first time I picked him up, due to his unexpectedly heavy head and shoulders. He almost tipped right out of my arms!

We had so much fun during the first few years of his life – camping, fishing, hiking – doing anything out of doors. On our first camping trip, I remember a chipmunk teasing Scout from the other side of the campfire. The chipmunk ran under the car and sat next to a tire. Scout ran around and around the car looking for that little guy but never finding him. Forever after, I'd imitate the sound of a chipmunk and Scout would come running.

I spent a lot of time while growing up walking with our first dog, Ranger in the woods of Northern Michigan. I came to love being outside, especially in the trees, on the trails and in local parks. With Scout, I also traveled these paths many times, something I still love to do. We made so many great memories when playing in the water, too. One time I taught Scout to jump off of our dock instead of just wading in at the shore. Of course, I had to jump off the dock first! As memory serves, I jumped five times before he finally took his first plunge, with Mom catching it all on camera. On the occasions that I had to leave Scout at home, I'd receive a unique greeting on my return: Scout would steal my hat off my head before I could even get out of the car. I lost count of how many baseball caps we eventually went through.

Then came a horrible day during our third summer. On the morning of June 21, 2012, a car hit my boy when he chased a cat across the road. He died instantly. My entire world changed. What began as a regular workday instantly transformed to the most horrible day of my life, with a phone call from my sister Lisa saying, "I don't think he made it." A state of shock set in.

"What the hell???!!!" ran through my head a million times. I had trained Scout to stay close to our house, and not cross the sidewalk. He never should have run into the street on his own. As the sole employee of the factory where I worked, I called my boss, shut down all the machinery, the lights, and the power, and left. I raced to the veterinarian's office in a weird dreamlike state of acceptance, anger, sadness, betrayal, and disbelief, all mixed together. I later learned that the driver of the car and quite a few other cars stopped and offered assistance or in the case of two nuns, knelt and prayed. My sister and the driver carried Scout to my sister's car, and she drove to the veterinary office near our house. Unfortunately (or thankfully, in hindsight), he had died instantly.

For the next few months, anger and sadness consumed me. My grief affected me so strongly that my mom researched and found Beyond the Paw Print Pet Loss Support Group. She suggested my sister and I attend a meeting. The idea of going to a support group frightened me. I hated public speaking, but my grief hurt so much, I knew I needed help.

When I think back on that initial BTPP meeting, the fact that I volunteered to be the first to speak showed how much I needed to get those feelings out in the open. Since that first meeting, I've realized how retelling that story has brought me a greater sense of awareness and comprehension. Every now and then, some tidbit surfaces that my memory has blocked, and I find myself sharing something new.

I also found it very helpful that Micky, the founder and facilitator of BTPP, allows space and time for each of us to express ourselves and share our story. Being among people who understand or have experienced this same pain helped me heal. The length of time for that healing varies for each person, as we're all different, and all on our own journey. I've grown immensely, and with Micky's guidance, wisdom, and friendship, have even become a member of the BTPP Advisory Board.

Through BTPP, I've made many new friends and I have learned how much I enjoy helping others. This may include assisting someone in a search for a new animal companion; others may choose to wait longer, if ever, before they find or accept the love of another companion. For me, life would be incomplete without animals.

During the drive to the vet's office on that horrid day, I already had thoughts of getting another dog. That might seem hasty, but fate took Scout, my very first puppy, way too soon. I had already spent too many years without a dog. As I thought back on my youth, Dad had tried to adopt puppies, but with our being so young, and the responsibilities on mom to care for them, it never quite worked out. When I was thirteen, Dad brought Ranger home, then a six-month-old Golden Retriever. While considered the family dog, he really belonged to me!

When I graduated from college, my single, working lifestyle, along with apartment life, didn't allow the time or space for a dog. In the years that followed, my sister Lisa and I moved into a house together, and I adopted my other sister's dog, Carmel. I had Carmel for seven years until cancer led to his passing. Finally, at the age of 45, I got my first puppy, Scout, only to lose him three a half years later.

Shortly after Scout's passing, I contacted his breeder to learn if she had any new puppies available for adoption. About three weeks later, we picked up my new Golden Retriever puppy, Casey. I named him after the main character from the baseball poem, *Casey at the Bat* written by Ernest Thayer. Calling our new dog Casey keeps my dad close and present in my heart since he loved this poem and I had come to love it as well. Little did I know that that phone call and the events that followed would lead me on a five-year journey, dedicated not just to Scout, but to all the dogs at that kennel.

I very much wanted Casey to become a therapy dog, so we tended to his training early. Most therapy groups require a dog to have reached the age of one year before becoming certified. Casey and I worked on our basics to become a well-mannered dog, capable of obeying the commands of sit, stay, down, and heel. He also needed to learn not to bark at other dogs and not to jump up on people.

As part of his training, I familiarized Casey with as many different people and situations as possible. We often used neighborhood home and garden supply stores as well as our township offices for practice. The Alliance of Therapy Dogs require no special training beyond a well-mannered canine who doesn't bark, jump up, or frighten easily, so we were already way ahead of the pack. I loved working with Casey, and he excelled as a student!

During this time, I also tried to find a second job at a doggie daycare facility and applied to at least five near my house. I got the same answer each time: no, due to my lack of experience. I had told Casey's breeder that she could call me if she ever needed kennel help since I could use some verifiable hours with the dogs. Not long after, we exchanged emails about a job and arranged for me to start working. That was the Friday after Memorial Day, June 2013.

Within the first couple of days, I recognized the horrible truth: My boys had come from a puppy mill. As the summer progressed, I learned the extent of this horrendous operation. I really could not believe or describe what I saw, so I began taking pictures. They showed the overcrowded and extremely unsanitary conditions which existed at the facility. My pictures also showed the lack of grooming as well as lack of dental and medical care for the dogs there. In order to determine a course of action, I showed my documentation to my vet, my mom's neighbor who volunteered with the Michigan Humane Society, and a county animal control officer.

Through my research, I learned about the Puppy Mill Awareness Group of Southeast Michigan. With the guidance, passion, and support of founder, Pam Sordyl, I filed a complaint with the Oakland County Animal Control in August 2013. I will not go into graphic details, but every day, when I left those dogs behind, their haunted eyes followed me, begging for help. Knowing that both Scout and Casey's parents and Scout's grandpa all still lived in that kennel increased my motivation to get that facility shut down. This motivation helped me to overcome my fear of public speaking.

With the help and encouragement of the BTPP attendees, my friend Pam, and especially Micky, I gained enough confidence to speak about this kennel many times. I did so in front of two city councils, at both the regular and committee meetings of the county commissioner, and even did two television interviews with a local news reporter. Through our efforts, along with other caring individuals, the state government passed the Large Breeder Registration Bill, which set standards and limits for dog breeders in Michigan. We persuaded the Oakland County commissioners to pass a resolution in support of this bill. Finally, after almost five years of battling, Oakland County Animal Control rescinded the kennel's license.

As a result of this remarkable journey, I have matured, grown, and changed in so many ways. I quit my job at the paper company and started my own small business, Karen 4-K9s, a specialized dog daycare with very limited boarding. I began working part-time at my vet's office as a kennel care assistant, and Casey and I gained the AKC's Canine Good Citizen title and passed our certification test for the group, the Alliance of Therapy Dogs. I am immensely proud of how far we've come.

Activity fills my new life with Casey, we do so much together. We volunteer weekly at an assisted living facility, visiting the residents and staff, and we compete along with my other dog, a German Shepherd named Gracie, in the fairly new dog sport of Canine Nose Work, a sport that imitates scent detection training used by drug or bomb-sniffing dogs. Canine Nose Work however uses essential oils, such as clove, anise, and birch, for the dogs to detect and locate. So far, we've competed in the Canine Works and Games and the United Kennel Club Nose Work trials. To honor Scout's memory, we use his collar as our "Start of Search" signal. At the beginning of every search, practice, or competition, I snap Scout's collar around either Casey or Gracie's neck and say, "Go find it."

I still think of Scout every day. He remains my soulmate, albeit one, sadly, with unfulfilled potential, and I miss him dearly. I treasure every picture and video of him and wish I had taken more. I decorated my bed with a pillowcase made from a favorite photo of him, and recently purchased a beautiful, 3-D, laser-engraved crystal rendering of my boy as well.

Most of the time I'm able to accept what happened to Scout, but I still have my bad days – on anniversaries, when I find an old medication in the cupboard, or when I receive a birthday club reminder in the mail. All these reminders can set me off balance. I know too that we made the most out of our short time together. Now, with the help of Micky along with past and present attendees of BTPP, I understand my emotions and recognize the many ways I have truly transformed my grief. I look forward to meeting all of my animal friends at the Rainbow Bridge.

Dedicated to Scout and the 58 Golden Retrievers from the puppy mill, among them Charger, Timmy, Goliath, Swinger (Scout's dad), Ohno (Casey's dad), Triscuit, Rugger, Rotor, Payton (Casey's grandpa), Patina (Casey's mom), Minor, A.J., Sophie, Marshmallow, Gumdrop, and Creampuff.

PABLO

STORY TWENTY TWO

Two Murmuring Hearts

By Micky

GROWING UP IN A RURAL LAKE COMMUNITY brought two gifts: a love and appreciation for the great outdoors and a devotion to the sweet barn cats who belonged to our next-door neighbor. There were few children in the community where we lived, and when my older siblings were busy, these cats often kept me company when I played outside. During the summer before sixth grade, I learned that we were leaving this community and moving to another home, near a mid-sized city. When I look back on that moment in time, I recall tearful goodbyes with the cats I had come to love as my own, the beautiful surroundings, and the sadness at leaving the first and only home I had known.

Time passed and with it brought many changes. Throughout the years of university life, travel, short-term teaching positions, further education, and subsequent moves, the opportunity just never felt right to adopt an animal companion of my own. Eventually, the opportunity presented itself when I returned home to Michigan to enter a Ph.D. program. It started with cat sitting for my neighbor Gary in the apartment complex where we both lived. His job required frequent travel, and he asked if I'd be interested in caring for his two cats during the times he'd be away from home. This request reminded me of how much I loved the neighbor cats from my youth. I was delighted to help Gary, and also to have the opportunity to learn about the care and nurturing of indoor cats. The other advantage of this arrangement: I developed the much-needed confidence to adopt my very own friend, and with that, my search for a companion began.

Over the months that followed, I met lots of adorable felines, both kittens and full-grown cats, at various shelters and venues, but something held me back from taking the next step. On an otherwise uneventful Valentine's Day in 1991, I scheduled a meet-and-greet at a local veterinary clinic that had kittens for adoption. The visit changed everything, and it all began with a gentle tap.

When I arrived, the assistant led me through the clinic toward a long narrow room with two levels of cages on both sides. The kittens were all together in a large cage on the lower level. As I was about to bend down to take a closer look at them, I felt a tap on my shoulder and heard a most adorable sound, demanding my attention: "Et eu, Et cu!" I turned around and saw a delicious, fat, gray and white paw, belonging to a gorgeous gray and white kitty, all alone in a big cage. Beautiful topaz eyes made direct contact with mine. This little kitty sure knew how to express himself! The loud purring and squawks of "Et eu," which I interpreted as kitty talk for "Hey you," had me love struck. It may sound silly, but I met the kitty squawks with a response of my own: "Are you the one who tapped my shoulder? You sure are a little sweetie and such a beauty. Whoever you belong to is so lucky!"

I turned to the assistant and said, "This is just the sort of kitty I've been looking for. What an adorable personality! I wish he or she were up for adoption."

"He is!" the assistant exclaimed. "We didn't mention him when you telephoned, because he has a heart murmur. We have to inform anyone interested in him of the potential veterinary bills that could be incurred, if he doesn't grow out of it." This information did not deter me. In fact, I felt a longing that I didn't quite understand. "He's four months old, but we're hopeful that someone will be charmed by his sweet disposition and adopt him." *Without missing a heartbeat*, I asked to hold him, and told the assistant that I too had been diagnosed with a heart murmur, "and I sure hope that won't prevent someone from loving me!"

As I looked into the kitty's eyes, I had no doubt that we were meant to be together … *two murmuring hearts*. As I held him, I felt pure joy. Love filled my own imperfect and lonesome heart. I knew without a doubt that we would heal each other's wounds. Might it have been more than a coincidence that I was able to bring him home on Valentine's Day? My heart says yes, that it was meant to be.

Choosing my new kitty's name was easy: I knew from the start that it would be Pablo. I had developed a fondness for the name during graduate school where among more practical worries —like finding a full-time teaching position and paying bills I also pondered the meaning of life and the meaning of love. One of my close classmates would attempt to inspire our fledgling crew of wannabe academics by sharing the work of one of his favorite poets, Pablo Neruda. During study breaks, I'd read Neruda's love poetry aloud as we discussed our lonely single existences. One of our favorite lines from the poem *Tonight I Can Write* served as inspiration for many of our late-night conversations: "Love is so short, forgetting is so long."

Little did I know that through the sixteen years and three months spent together with Pablo, I would learn the most important lesson of my life: Love wasn't something to be feared, and it doesn't have to hurt. I learned from this adored kitty that I could love and be loved unconditionally. How lucky was I to be the recipient of his loyal devotion? I often joyfully reflect on our introduction and feel so fortunate that Pablo chose me to be his guardian. This little guy trusted me to care for him and I didn't take that covenant lightly. A gentle, sweet soul, he was as devoted to me as I was to him. As I reflected on the line from Neruda's poem, I understood that although love might indeed be short, I consider myself very fortunate that Pablo lived for sixteen years and three months. Our time together lasted longer than most human relationships!

There are so many happy memories. I remember how, in anticipation of bringing Pablo home, I excitedly prepped my apartment with everything a kitty required. Nothing but the very best litter box would suffice, kitty food and bowls, toys and more toys! I had someone to love and someone to mother. Beyond the fun stuff, I knew I needed to find a veterinary office closer to home to care for this special little guy and his heart murmur. After receiving a multitude of recommendations for a nearby practice, I made an appointment. As we waited in the exam room at our first visit, Pablo meowed loudly and moved nervously along the edges of the exam table attempting to find a way out. As a new mom, I wasn't sure how to soothe him. He easily escaped my arms, jumped to the floor, and proceeded to stand on his hind legs and pound the door with soft kitty paws. I reassured Pablo that all would be well and held him close while we waited to meet our new vet. He wasn't the only one in the room who was anxious: I had numerous questions about his heart murmur.

A few minutes later, the vet entered the exam room accompanied by his nurse Leslie, and with a big smile and bigger-than-life voice, said, "Hello gorgeous!" Feeling myself blush, I thought, "Wow, that's a first! I've never received a greeting like this in all my life!" Within seconds, I realized he was talking to Pablo! I quickly recovered and heartily agreed that my boy was indeed one gorgeous kitty. Through this visit, the doctor reassured us that with the proper care, Pablo had a good long life ahead of him. That first visit led to a friendship with our vet, his wife, and children that has spanned 27 years.

Pablo was easy to leash train, which meant we could take short walks within the apartment complex where we lived or enjoy short rides in the car. We would often visit my mom or dad, and on a few occasions, Pablo accompanied me to the home of my doctoral dissertation adviser to pick up yet another red-marked version with demands for further rewrites. His presence lifted my spirits as I prepared for further writing! Drivers often smiled and waved when they would see Pablo lounging casually across the dashboard, without a care in the world.

I also purchased a papoose, or baby carrier, at a local mother and baby store. I didn't dare tell the sales associate that I wasn't buying it for a pregnant relative, but for my kitten. If it sounds a bit nutty, it was! Carrying Pablo in the papoose allowed me to take him to the local pet stores, where he could look at the fish swimming in the store aquariums and the pretty birds singing songs from their cages. Amazingly, he never tried to leap out. He appeared happy to observe his fellow creatures from the safety of my arms.

We had a true relationship of mutual adoration. Little Pablo would lay in front of the door every morning as if to say, "Mom, don't go!" As this became a daily pattern, I realized I needed to find a special friend to keep him company for the long hours I was at school, at the library, or teaching at the university.

Through our vet's office, I learned about a litter of kitties that had been brought into a nearby clinic. As I drove there, my expectations were low: I didn't think I'd find a love match on the very first day of my search. How wrong I was! I returned home with a muted Calico who had a mark over her left eye that resembled a horseshoe. I was hoping to adopt a female and this little lady stood out immediately with her confident, bossy manner. Her special mark also made me think she might just bring our little home a dose of good luck.

Despite her loud squawks, the kitty turned out to be very sweet, and I thought she'd make the perfect match for Pablo and his gentle temperament. She did: Isabella (named after an actress I admired) ruled the roost from her first day to her last. Our home was complete, and I no longer worried about Pablo being alone while I was gone all day as he and Isabella bonded within the first 24 hours.

The following spring, I was nearing the end of my coursework and narrowing down my dissertation topic. The task was arduous for me and I was grateful for the company of my Pablo and Isabella during the many hours I'd spent studying and writing at home. One afternoon, my mom surprised me with a visit and lunch. It made me incredibly happy when either of my parents would stop over, and that day was no exception. My mom suggested we go for a walk within the apartment complex, seeing that it was a beautiful spring day. During our outing, a sweet little black kitty strolled out of the nearby woods. Her facial features were truly *aristocatic*, and her big green eyes were gorgeous. As I stopped to pet this friendly feline, my mom took one look and said, "Oh no, don't even think about it. Two cats are fine, but a third will get everyone talking!"

ISABELLA

"Don't worry," I told her, "if she's around the next time I go for a walk, I'll take her to the vet's office to see if they can put her up for adoption." The very next morning I drove to the same wooded area and softly called out, "Kitty, kitty." She immediately came out of the woods and allowed me to hold her, just as she had the previous day. She had surely been abandoned as she appeared very thin and lonesome.

Purring all the while, she allowed me to hold her and was very compliant when I placed her in the cat carrier I'd brought along. Fortunately, it was a short drive to my veterinarian where I asked that she be given a complete physical. At the office, they asked if I planned to adopt her. I explained that I had no plans to take in a third companion, but would put up signs throughout the apartment complex to learn if anyone had a missing cat. I reassured the staff that I would be glad to pay for her boarding fees until a home could be found.

After a couple days, no one had responded to my posters and no one else had shown an interest in adopting her. One week turned into two, and finally on the third week, I returned to the vet to visit the mystery kitty. When Leslie, the nurse, brought her out for me to hold, the kitty held her paw up to my cheek and caressed it while purring loudly. That was the ***cat***alyst! "I'm taking her home and I'm naming her Nellie!" Her name was chosen on the spot, just like my decision to bring her home.

To say we had an interesting adjustment period is an understatement. The tranquility of life with Pablo and Isabella changed in an instant! The new addition to our household caused tremendous upheaval, despite following all the instructions provided by our vet. Eventually, after a few months, everyone began to calm down and our household changed from combat zone to a tentative Armistice.

I felt loved by all three of these unique and special beings, and through them learned how to care for someone other than myself. The affection I received from Pablo and the girls led me to hope that I might be a lovable person. This was a tremendous breakthrough for me, someone who has had a lifelong struggle with low self-esteem, along with hefty doses of anxiety and depression as the icing on the top of my cake of personal struggles. Between the professional help I received for these struggles, the support of my parents, along with the love of these kitties, I slowly began to feel a bit of optimism for the future. The companionship of these three adored cats opened the door for hope to enter. Amazing, isn't it? I wouldn't have believed it possible, but it's true. *It wasn't their love alone that helped*, but without it, I'm not certain I would have been ready for the next phase of my life.

NELLIE

Eventually, I began to imagine that perhaps I might be ready for a two-legged life partner of my own. Pablo, with his harem of two, generously shared me with the man I met and eventually married in 1997, the human version of this gentle soul. Once again, my cat loving neighbor Gary, brought joy into my life, as he introduced me to the man who would become the love of my life. Who would have imagined how one connection would lead to another, and that my life would be changed in the process?

In the writing of this story, I've discovered the significance of these connections and feel immense gratitude for all the twists and turns of my journey. On the occasions that I struggled, my mom often said, "when God closes a door, he opens a window," and throughout my life I found her favorite saying to be true. And the love of three amazing companions sure did soften some of my defenses, which helped me believe in life's possibilities.

From the moment my husband and I met, I understood that he possessed rare qualities that I had come to appreciate through my dear Pablo: sweetness, devotion, exquisite listening skills, patience, loyalty, a fun-loving disposition, the ability to live in the present, a discerning appetite, great looks, and a sassy chassis! Most of all, this gentleman was a lover of all animals. I had hit the jackpot! Then came an unexpected yet exciting hurdle.

My fiancé was offered an overseas assignment by his employer and would be moving to England for a minimum of three years. Even more exciting: I was to join him in that wonderful country after our wedding. There was never a question about whether the cats would come along; in fact, they were part of my then-fiancé's relocation package. I was so grateful that we would be starting our married life with our three kitties in this overseas adventure; it was more than I could have ever imagined. How did this ordinary girl with her big bag of emotional troubles find this kind of real-life love story? The next part of our journey was about to begin.

Three years turned into seven and the kitties thrived along with their mum and pop. However, there was one occasion where Pablo took matters into his own paws and gave us quite a scare. In preparation for a business trip we were both going to take, I sought the help of our favorite cat nanny. She was unavailable on the dates we'd be away, so the pet-sitting agency suggested I meet another candidate to care for Pablo, Nellie, and Isabella. She arrived at the appointed time and we began the interview. As we conversed, I didn't feel a love connection, but I assumed this was a result of my high expectations. As part of familiarizing her with the kitties and their care, I explained that as indoor cats, they were very curious about the great outdoors. I explained how being a little mischievous, they often attempted to slip out our front door whenever we entered or exited. As a result, we were always extra cautious to ensure they were safe and sound inside our home.

With repeated assurances of, "You shouldn't worry, I've never lost a cat," I phoned the agency and agreed to hire this woman for our time away. In hindsight, I should have paid more attention to Pablo's unique reaction when I attempted to wake him from his nap in his favorite basket. He opened his eyes, took a brief look at our guest, and then promptly shut them. Despite my gentle coaxing, he wasn't interested. I didn't think too much about his apparent dislike for this stranger who, unbeknownst to him, was going to be in charge of his care and take over his home. However, once we departed and the cat nanny stepped in, *Pablo wasn't having it*: On the second day of her stay, he escaped out the front door when she was entering our apartment. Unfortunately, she didn't see that he had gotten out, and didn't notice his absence until the evening when he was due for his medication that controlled his seizures. When I phoned the next day to learn how the kitties were coping with their temporary guardian and vice versa, I received the news: Pablo was missing.

I was hysterical with worry. Pablo was a sweet and gentle indoor cat, with a health condition that required medication. Moreover, we were unable to return for another two days. The sitter enlisted the help of the Diplomatic Protection Officers who guarded the nearby Kensington Palace to which our building was connected, an old army barracks which had been converted to apartments. Despite all efforts, there were no sightings or signs of Pablo. On the second day of his absence, one of the officers suggested that the sitter place his food and water bowls near the apartment entryway behind the shrubs. He might find cover and safety there and be attracted to the food should he try to come home.

Gratefully, the sitter complied with their suggestion. When she checked on the bowls later that evening, she saw that the food was gone. Praying it was Pablo and not another creature, we all began to feel a shred of hope. The bowls were refilled that night. The next morning the food bowl was empty again. This time, the sitter decided to search the shrubs surrounding the building. Lo and behold, she found Pablo snoozing in the sun, protected from view and harm by the landscaping.

This was one lucky cat sitter. To be fair, she had done her best and had even conducted daily searches with other colleagues who had pet sitting jobs in the area. She rightfully credited the Diplomatic Protection Officers for their ongoing help and advice for the successful discovery and rescue of our beloved Pablo. His adventure resulted in three of the most distressing and frightening days I had as his mom.

We couldn't wait to return home to see Pablo with our own eyes and to hold him close. After a trip to the vet's office to treat cuts on his paws, all was well. We delivered thank you baskets to the officers, full of teas and tasty treats procured from a favorite London emporium, with a note from Pablo, thanking them for their role in his rescue. Much to our delight, we received a note of thanks from the Diplomatic Protection Group which we continue to treasure all these many years later. I have excerpted the following portion of the letter which was addressed to Pablo:

Dear Pablo,

Thank you very much indeed for the thoughtful gift from Fortnum & Mason. We are all glad to hear that your adventure turned out well in the end and we also hope that it won't be repeated too often, too soon. At least if you do decide to go exploring again, we all now know where you live and how much your parents want you back, safe and well. Could you please pass on to Bud and Micky all our best wishes and thanks for helping you spend your allowance on such a generous token of appreciation.

With sincerest thanks,
All the troops at Kensington DPG Base

I am grateful to report that this was the one and only great adventure had by Pablo for the duration of the time we lived in England. We were so happy to have our boy back, and realized how fortunate we were for the safe return of my very best, treasured friend.

On our repatriation to Michigan, Pablo lived another five years, however, the last two of his life weren't easy. With various ailments already, his heart murmur being one, Pablo was diagnosed with end-stage kidney disease which was treated with fluids injected through an IV to keep him hydrated. As the disease progressed, so did the frequency of fluid treatments. Eventually, it all became too much for his heart. Everything changed in an instant.

The evening of March 28, 2008 was an otherwise typical one for us. As we prepared for sleep, Pablo came up on the bed, using the step stool we kept at the bedside. He settled down next to me and all appeared well until 3:00 a.m. when we woke to hear him howling in pain. We quickly realized the severity of the

situation and that we needed to take action immediately.
We wrapped him in his blanket as gently as possible and drove to the emergency veterinary hospital. After a brief stop by a police officer for speeding, we continued along the highway, hoping that the vet staff could stop the pain. We also realized that Pablo might not survive this latest development. Through my tears and fear, I held my boy closely and told him how much I loved him, over and over. I thanked him repeatedly for his sweet and gentle devotion and apologized for being unable to stop the pain. After a brief exam, the emergency vet told us that we had to say goodbye, immediately. With Pablo in our arms, he was euthanized. It was the only answer to his suffering. As he was taking his last breaths, we reassured him that all would be well and he would be joining his beloved Nellie who had gone to her rest, one month earlier. The two of them would soon be frolicking together, among all the other heavenly creatures, happy and free of pain.

When my husband and I finally felt prepared to leave the emergency center, a technician handed us a special memento: Pablo's paw print with his name written above it surrounded by hearts. It was a lovely and fitting gesture. When I shared the news with our family veterinary office, they sent flowers, a card, and a donation in Pablo's name to a local animal charity. In addition, a vet specialist who had provided palliative care for Pablo's various senior maladies through non-traditional modalities such as acupuncture and Chinese remedies, also sent a card and made herself available over the phone. I was grateful for the validation and recognition of Pablo's life through the veterinary community.

I soon discovered that *beyond the paw print* memento and the kindness of these veterinary practices, otherwise caring people in our circle of family and friends were fairly unsympathetic, or perhaps, uncertain how to respond to my grief. Some of the reactions led me to wonder if mourning the death of an animal simply wasn't perceived as legitimate or "normal." For example, one month prior to Pablo's passing, on February 29 (leap year), 2008, we had to say goodbye to Nellie, who herself had been experiencing a variety of serious senior cat maladies. Their end-of-life story was eerily similar. Both were unexpected emergency situations occurring in the middle of the night that required immediate action. These unusual circumstances compelled me to share their stories with others. *Bad idea.* I soon learned that in some situations, and with some people, it was best if I avoided the subject altogether.

When Pablo and Nellie were alive, I was blissfully unaware that there were people who didn't understand pet loss grief. In reflection, I'm not sure what I expected, or what I wanted at the time of their passing, but I knew it wasn't what I often heard: "What's wrong with you?" ... "It's been a week (or two) already, it's time to move on!" ... "It was just a cat. Go to a shelter and adopt a new one!" So, I grieved privately, handling activities of daily living and other responsibilities without any discussion of the losses of Pablo and Nellie. In my interactions with the outside world, it was as though they never existed. This felt terrible. Did I expect a brass band and parade through town, flags flown at half mast, or a 21-gun salute? No, of course not, I was merely hoping to openly mourn the deaths of my beloved companions without fear of judgment or ridicule.

Through my academic mentor, Dr. Kelly Rhoades, and other writers on pet loss grief, I learned to control my desire to pass judgment on those who judged me. After all, each of us hurts in some way from something.

When it came time to say goodbye to Isabella seven months later, we mourned only with our friends at the veterinary practice. I didn't know how to deal with all this grief, but my persistent, recurring thought was that there had to be others experiencing similar struggles, and if so, I wanted to meet them. The loss of our three beloved companions and the stress of holding my grief inside reinforced the feeling that I needed additional support. *At the time, it never occurred to me that I would be the one to provide it … for others.* I could see that there was a void that needed to be filled with a special form of support: a pet loss support group.

They say timing is everything in life, and the course of events that followed supported the veracity of that saying. I was in the midst of a graduate program in Hospice and Palliative studies at the time that Nellie, Pablo, and Isabella died. With the encouragement of Dr. Rhoades, the department chairperson, I changed the direction of my research and focused on the subject of pet loss grief. From one semester to the next, I studied various aspects of this topic and a dream became a reality. I was inspired to create, Beyond the Paw Print Pet Loss Support Group with the slogan "Transforming Our Grief Beyond the Paw Print." I had a strong desire to bring together like-minded individuals who had grieved in isolation, just as I had.

With the support of local veterinarians, word-of-mouth recommendations, and local newspaper coverage, BTPP has developed a niche, serving those traveling the unfamiliar terrain of pet loss grief. My hopes and objectives are for attendees to find a safe, confidential space, where stories are shared and validated in a warm, caring, and supportive atmosphere. Another objective is to provide something that eluded me in the early days of my grieving over the passing of my three beloved cats – resources! As a result, each meeting has a table with a variety of books, brochures, and handouts on the subject of pet loss, grief, and healing.

I am very grateful that something meaningful has resulted from the lives and deaths of Pablo, Nellie, and Isabella. This story is my love letter to them. Their lives changed mine, and BTPP is their legacy. I have learned through my own experience, and that of the courageous individuals who have attended the meetings, that if we are willing, grief can transform our lives. I can hardly believe that it all started twenty-seven years ago, with a tap on the shoulder, and *the murmuring of two hearts.*

In memory of all the other animal companions I have known and loved including my first childhood pets, turtles Herman and Henry; a multitude of goldfish; the barnyard cats; for a brief interlude, our sweet poodle, Jacques; and most recently, our dear sweet feline, Kensington.

With gratitude to Mother Nature and all the amazing creatures, whose appearance along the nature trails where I walk elicit emotions of sheer wonder and joy.

DARREN

Afterword

By Patty Merlo, M.P.M.

I KNOW THAT MY HEART HAS BEEN FOREVER CHANGED after reading these stories of love, loss, and lessons learned. I hope the same may be true for you as well. It was truly a privilege to read heartfelt tales that reveal the deep bond and connection between humans and their beloved companion animals.

I noticed that a common theme in each story is the gratitude expressed for the way a companion unabashedly offers unconditional love and joy – at the mere sight of their guardian. Regardless of appearance, bank account, politics, or religion, we are loved, comforted, and consoled through all of life's ups and downs by our devoted companions. When a death cuts short this flow of pure, unconditional emotion, it is natural to grieve deeply.

The loss of our adored companions can evoke a variety of emotions: sadness, loneliness, hopelessness, anger, frustration, regret, and guilt. One might feel inconsolable one minute, then relieved in the next moment that the suffering of an animal companion has ended. The grief may be complicated with the feeling that you didn't do enough for them, a sweet animal who relied on you for their care.

Self-doubt associated with pet loss is familiar to me since I too had to say goodbye to my beloved canine companion, Darren. I remember the deep ache in my heart when others were unable to understand or support my grief.

Given my own experience, I found huge consolation when I attended Beyond the Paw Print meetings. There, I had the privilege of meeting and listening to a multitude of attendees as they worked their way from grief toward healing. Additionally, over the ten years that BTPP has existed, Micky has also entrusted me to facilitate meetings when circumstances called her away.

In fact, Micky and I met while enrolled in a graduate program in hospice and bereavement studies. We had a natural connection since both of us were on a journey to better understand the process of grief, loss, and healing. After graduation, in my role as chaplain or spiritual director, I began leading retreats and meeting with individuals on the topics of spirituality, forgiveness, and prayer. This work unexpectedly revealed that many people remain stuck in their grief – unable to make peace with or reconcile their human losses.

When I read the stories in this book, I was struck to find that the participants expressed similar struggles with their own grief over the death of their animal companions. This discovery led me to think about how I might be of assistance. Is there something from my experience that may be helpful? So, when Micky asked me to write this afterword, I immediately said yes. As I began to write, the words seemed to flow from my heart. My hope is that the following thoughts on self-compassion, self-forgiveness, along with a guided meditation, bring some comfort for your hurting heart.

In judging ourselves harshly, we forget that making mistakes is a part of our common humanity. None of us are perfect, although the voice inside us often expects us to be!

In your grief, you may forget to offer yourself the same understanding, or self-forgiveness, that you received from your animal companions. From there, it is easy to fall into the trap of judging yourself harshly. What can become harmful, even self-destructive, is ruminating over all the things you believe you did "wrong." Repeatedly berating yourself for "not doing enough" or criticizing yourself with thoughts of "I should have…" or "I could have…" can lead to physical and emotional distress.

I would like you to consider a different way of reflecting on your loss. Might it be possible to let go of self-criticism? How about creating a new legacy? If you're willing, I'm asking that you take a moment to recall:

- The positive ways you have been changed by the unconditional love of your companion.
- Reflect on the many wonderful memories you shared.
- Remember the many ways you expressed love for your companion during his or her lifetime.

Perhaps you might honor their memory by being the person they believed you to be: loving and caring. It might seem impossible in the aftermath of a loss, but you have the ability to bring these characteristics out in yourself. This form of self-care can begin with two practices: self-compassion and self-forgiveness. Together these practices make it possible to love yourself as you were loved by your animal companion:

- Begin by acknowledging all your feelings (remember that none are "good" or "bad").
- Speak gently to yourself as you would to a friend who lost a beloved animal companion.
- Treat yourself with kindness as this lays the groundwork for accepting the circumstances that occurred at the time of your pet's passing. Repeating the phrase, "I did the best I could at the time" can quiet the voice of self-criticism and lessen the intensity of painful feelings.

Along with nurturing self-forgiveness and self-compassion, there is another aid I've acquired during my time as a chaplain and spiritual director: I began to incorporate guided meditations as part of my work, and was grateful to see the comfort they bring to people who are grieving. As a way to conclude this book of love, loss, and lessons learned, I felt compelled to create this guided meditation especially for you. May it help bring some light to your hurting heart as you work your way through grief toward healing.

Note: Ideally, I would like for you to listen to the following meditation, which will allow you to absorb the message with your eyes closed. If possible, ask a trusted, caring person in your life to slowly and gently read this meditation aloud. Alternatively, visit our website, www.beyondthepawprint.com and click on the meditation tab. These two options allow you to fully enjoy the benefits of the entire meditation, with your eyes closed. Or, if you prefer, read the meditation, silently, in the order in which it is presented below.

GUIDED MEDITATION

1. Before beginning this meditation, ensure that you'll have ten to fifteen minutes of uninterrupted quiet.

2. You may wish to put on some comfortable clothing — though that's not necessary.

3. Gather together special mementos that remind you of your beloved companion — photos, toys, or collar.

4. Sit in a comfortable chair, sofa, or a cozy corner on the floor amidst pillows and a light blanket.

5. Take three slow deep breaths, one at a time. If the situation allows, gently close your eyes.

6. Take a moment to notice your body. Notice where there might be tension or tightness, perhaps in your shoulders or your jaw, gently allow it to soften and release. And now, notice your breathing. There's no need to change or shift, just notice how wonderfully your body takes in life-giving oxygen, all on its own. And then notice as you breathe out, how your body prepares for the next breath. Spend a moment or two and just notice this everyday miracle.

7. Now take one more nice deep breath. And this time, allow any remaining tension to flow out of you, as you exhale.

8. When you feel ready, imagine yourself in a place where you and your beloved companion (say his or her name) would most enjoy being together. Can you remember a specific time?

9. Maybe you will "see" and feel the special memory, where you were, the colors around you, the feel of their fur, the sounds that surround you. Were others with you? Or was it just the two of you? Perhaps you were outside with your companion or curled up in a favorite spot indoors? Just rest in that wonderful memory for a moment. You may even notice a smile coming to your face as you remember, or you may notice a soft tear.

10. Allow as much time as you like with the feelings and memories of the companionship and tender moments you shared. Feel your own heart softening and opening, warm and tender, filled with love and happiness. You may see them running to greet you, or pressing up against you, or you may hear their excited greeting as they welcome you.

11. Perhaps there is something you would like your companion to know, something you would like to share with them.

12. You might express how much you miss your companion (name) and how grateful you are for the time you had together, how deeply changed (for the better!) you are because of your companion's devotion and love.

13. Spend some time with those memories, both the happy times and, if you are ready, the more poignant moments as well.

14. Express any regrets and ask forgiveness from your companion (name) for unintended mistakes or hurtful choices made.

15. Sometimes it can be too painful to speak directly to a loved one whom you believe you have hurt by word or action. If you feel overwhelmed by sadness and regret, think of a trusted friend/caring other and the support they might offer you through this guided meditation. All that is required of this special friend, or even another animal, is that they have known and loved your companion. Imagine this friend or animal sitting comfortably beside you, a loving presence.

16. Be sure to allow enough time for silence, for simply being together, recalling the special behaviors or habits that you loved during the times you were together.

17. The passage over the Rainbow Bridge may have given your companion (name) a deeper level of compassion, love and forgiveness. Your beloved companion (name) may wish to share some lessons learned on the other side of the Rainbow Bridge. Silently ask if your companion (name) has a message they would like to share with you. Allow yourself to receive these messages through your various senses, which may include sight, sound, or physical sensation.

18. Thank your companion (by name) for being a part of your life.

19. Thank your companion (by name) for all the lessons learned.

20. Thank your companion (by name) for one of the most important lessons of all: That you are lovable.

21. Before saying goodbye to your companion, you may wish to use your imagination one more time.

22. If you are ready, imagine yourself opening your arms and releasing your companion.

23. In this moment, you are recognizing that it is time for your companion to cross back over the Rainbow Bridge.

24. Even though they may go, all the feelings of love and care remain as you recognize that your companion is on his or her own journey toward peace and well-being, where all is and will remain well, where your companion is forever safe and loved by a force greater than our own understanding.

25. Might you recognize that you too are loved, by that same force, a love that will hold you and carry you?

26. When you're ready, begin to bring yourself back to the present, slowly, and in your own time.

27. Take three slow, deep breaths. Wiggle your fingers and toes. When you feel ready, slowly open your eyes.

28. Allow yourself to savor the happy memories of the love you received from your companion. Invite those memories to remain with you.

29. Hug yourself and make a conscious intention to spread love and kindness to those within your present circle or extend it further to those you may encounter in your daily routine.

30. May you discover that peace and well-being are within reach, as you continue your journey toward healing.

Preparing for Your Pet's End-of-Life Journey

By Dr. Ellen LaFramboise

As a pet parent, receiving a terminal diagnosis for your animal is devastating. In the ER, I often had to deliver the bad news to otherwise unsuspecting families. In these situations, you may only process about 30 percent of the message being delivered, since your emotion clouds your ability to hear the news. You may only have ten or fifteen minutes with the vet to listen and discuss the diagnosis, prognosis and the plan of care. It may be difficult to know what questions to ask, especially if the diagnosis was unexpected. However, if your pet's situation isn't urgent, follow up with your veterinarian to discuss the diagnosis and a treatment plan. This will also give you time to make a list of questions in preparation for the next appointment.

This may be a good time to consider adding a hospice veterinarian to your pet's care team. Even if you are seeking treatment (like surgery or chemotherapy for cancer), a hospice vet can help support both your pet and your family, focusing on making their life as comfortable as possible. Because of this approach, families often tell me that their pet is doing better than before the diagnosis.

During follow-up appointments with your veterinarian or hospice care-giver, make sure to discuss all the treatment options that are available. Making the right decision for your pet means understanding the treatment, the goals of the treatment, possible side effects or recovery times, the length of commitment on your part, and the costs involved. If possible, request that a friend or family member participate in these discussions to ease the burden of conveying medical information to those who weren't there.

If you should choose to pursue hospice support for your pet, please understand that this isn't giving up, as many think it is. Education is the key in hospice care. I find that most of my families feel relief after our first meeting because they've acquired information on what to expect and how to make decisions for their beloved pet. A good hospice vet will teach you how to assess your pet's quality of life.

There are many things that the family can do during the end of life phase to make it more meaningful. I recommend making a list of all the things your dog or cat loves to do. Can they still do any of them? If so, make sure these are daily occurrences. Could an activity be modified so that it can still bring them joy? For dogs who have trouble on their regular walks, I recommend "senior wanders." Just getting outside in the fresh air and getting to sniff some trees close to the house can be very enjoyable. Listen to and observe your pet when it comes to their comfort level with outdoor walks. For pets with significant weakness or mobility problems, a wagon or cart can help them easily get out of the house.

Consider making a bucket list for your pet. Did they always love the beach? Do they have a favorite hiking trail? Do they prefer just snuggling on the couch? This is the time to try to organize outings or events that will create wonderful memories for you and fantastic experiences for your pet. Social pets may love a party in their honor. Be creative! While you're at it, take lots of pictures. These are some of my most treasured memories from my pets. Consider hiring a photographer and having a photo shoot to capture some special images. All of these things will help your pet to live on in your heart after they are gone.

WHEN THE TIME COMES TO SAY GOODBYE

"You'll know when it's time" is a phrase too often uttered when it comes to the loss of our beloved animals. I disagree and very much avoid saying it to pet families. This statement implies that there is only one "right" time to help our pet pass peacefully. That's simply not true. As a veterinarian, I may be able to tell, medically, when it is time. But as a member of the pet's family, it's very hard to know. Choosing a peaceful passing begins at the time of a terminal diagnosis and ends when the pet enters a crisis and we have lost the ability to choose.

Every time I have had to make the decision to help one of my own pet's pass, I've struggled with it—and I'm supposed to be the expert! The choice to euthanize rarely feels right. For many, it is an immensely difficult decision. A multitude of factors impact our reactions, including, but not limited to, our past experiences with death and loss, our relationship to the pet, our own expectations on how things should occur, and the support that we may or may not receive from friends and family.

If euthanasia isn't the right choice for your family to make, it is best to seek out the support of a hospice veterinarian. They have training in hospice supported natural death and can be there to make sure your pet is comfortable through to the end. They will also work to educate the family on how to care for a pet through this stage of life and what to expect as death progresses.

You may want to think about what is important for you and your pet at this time. Will you choose to be at your veterinarian's office, or would you like for your pet to pass at home? Who do you want to be there? If you have young children, is it right for them to be there? For in-home euthanasia, is there a special place where your pet is most comfortable? Would you like to light candles or play comforting music? You may even elect to have a celebration of life and invite those who have loved your pet to be there at the end. One of the most special experiences I've had was during a visit to help two very old dogs who were siblings pass together. The family had a printed program that included prayers and songs that were part of this experience. The extended family was there to say their goodbyes. It certainly brought me to tears.

Acknowledgements

By Micky Golden Moore

MY ACKNOWLEDGEMENTS BEGIN WITH every individual who attended a Beyond the Paw Print (BTPP) meeting. Our sessions have been a classroom where together we have learned about this multifaceted, unavoidable, wild terrain of this thing called grief. Through open listening, acknowledgement, validation, kindness, and kinship toward one another, attendees have given each other the space to make their way toward healing. As the facilitator of these meetings, I have developed a deeper appreciation of the human — animal companion bond. As a result of the many individuals who have shared their stories at a meeting, I have found the courage to share my stories of the love and loss of my adored animal companions, Pablo, Isabella and Nellie. Additionally, listening to the stories that have been shared in this group has shaped how I support attendees through their loss. Quite simply, this group has changed and enriched my life in more ways than I ever could have imagined.

I am forever grateful to the twenty-one individuals who agreed to participate in this project. The stories of love, loss, and healing, so bravely shared at the meetings, are now part of a broader reach, so that others who might be grieving in isolation, are now beneficiaries of their wisdom and growth.

Thank you: Brady, Carol, Charlene, Diana, Ellen, Ian, Jackie, Jake, Jill, Karen, Kate, Kristine, Laura, Lindsay, Marlene, Mary Anne, Mary Ellen, Ric (and Paula), Shari, Steve, and Sue for joining me in this project. Without their participation, this book would not exist. They willingly revisited happy times along with painful memories in order to share the life stories of their animal companions in this book. I consider each contributor a dear friend and cohort on the journey toward healing.

When BTPP was in its formative stages, I recall brainstorming potential meeting locations. Finding the right environment for the BTPP meetings took several months and was an adventure in and of itself. I had reached out to several venues with great trepidation, uncertain of the response I would receive when I described my idea for a pet loss support group. I toured a variety of spaces, but none felt right. Then I found the perfect place, and it was less than one mile from our home. From my initial inquiry, church administrator Linda Hall, Pastor Carol (through 2015), and staff of the Orchard United Methodist Church of Farmington Hills were kind and welcoming. Linda's response served to further enhance my confidence, and after touring this special church, I knew I had found the right home for my group. Since Pastor Carol's retirement, Pastor Amy has been equally supportive of BTPP. I am so grateful for the continuing kindness of the staff. We feel safe and supported within this beautiful space.

One of the unexpected benefits of facilitating BTPP meetings, in person and online, has been the opportunity to encounter truly wonderful people, and in some cases, form lasting friendships. Karen Irwin began attending BTPP meetings in 2012, first to receive support (read about Karen's dog Scout, in story 21), later to offer support to new attendees. Karen is now a BTPP Advisory Board member and trusted colleague.

Dr. Ellen Laframboise, founder of Crossroads Veterinary Hospice, reached out to BTPP, when she sought information about the group for her grieving clients. In recent years, Ellen has returned to BTPP as a presenter to educate the audience about veterinary hospice care. I never anticipated that I would be in need of Ellen's services until the day our cat, Kensington became gravely ill on December 26, 2017. Ellen's composed, caring, and professional demeanor were exactly what we needed as we prepared to say goodbye to our boy. I am grateful that Ellen agreed to share Austin's story (Story 20), along with her guidelines for guardians facing end of life decisions located in the Appendix section of this book.

The BTPP Pet Loss Support Group was launched on Facebook in 2008 and has members across the globe. Stories are shared, photos are posted, and an abundance of support is provided among members. There are many individuals who retain their membership in order to support new members. Yes, long after their wounds have softened, these individuals have remained active in the group. Their participation is greatly appreciated, and their insights are invaluable. Thank you to the following online BTPP members, whose participation spans nearly five or more years: Carol Bartley, Dennis Cole, Patti Cole, Renee Edmunds, Debbie Glen, Katie Gordon, Kathryn Holloway, Lisa Irwin, Susan Johnson, Marlene Konkoly, Lois Paquin-Hoffiz, Pam Varcoe Miller, Shelly Molnar, Tricia Stehle, David Whitten.

Kayla Stomack, DVM learned about my group through a vet tech who joined her practice. She divides her time between Advanced Animal Emergency in Clinton Township and Lap of Love, a nationwide team of mobile vets providing hospice care at home. Many thanks to Dr. Stomack for her support of BTPP and her efforts to arrange additional meetings throughout the greater Detroit area.

Lois Raitt generously volunteers as my associate facilitator of the online BTPP Facebook group. Her dedication, passion, and desire to support those grieving the death of their animal companions has surpassed all expectations. I am fortunate that BTPP brought us together. Lois has generously supported online members without seeking recognition for her efforts.

Many thanks to Dr. David Whitten and his associate, Dr. Cindy Atler, both of Hilldale Veterinary Hospital. Together they provided excellent care for Pablo, Isabella, Nellie, and Kensington. From birth through goodbye, they were there through it all. The journey continues with Cornwall and Chelsea. In addition to providing all-around excellent care, they educated us on how to be the best possible parents to our beloved feline companions.

As our feline companions became familiar with the staff at Hilldale, I had the privilege of becoming acquainted with Dr Whitten, his wife Susan, and their entire family. I am so happy for the friendship that developed with Dr. Dave and Susan Whitten and their five children, now grown with spouses and families of their own: *Kiirsti* and Don Sharp, *Amanda* and Matthew Gittleson, *Emily* and Joe Abid, *Aaron* & Lindsay Whitten, and *Andy* & Kristina Whitten. Kiirsti, Emily and Amanda have been ports in the storm through it all. I treasure their friendship and love them dearly.

I am especially grateful that Dr. Whitten and daughters Kiirsti, Amanda, and Emily attended BTPP meetings in the early years, lending support and insight to grieving pet owners. Their ongoing referrals to BTPP are much appreciated. What better compliment could there be? What would a veterinary practice be without the caring nurses who greet nervous guardians and their companions? Thank you to Pablo, Nellie and Isabella's favorite veterinary nurse, now retired, Leslie Lakits Swayze. Leslie cared for our animal companions with genuine love and tenderness; She is greatly missed.

In the summer of 2007, the Carlson family (Dennis, Mary Lynn, Tim and Kristin) moved into the home across the street. A relationship formed when Mary Lynn Carlson promoted her son Tim's computer care and repair business by putting flyers in the mailboxes of neighbors. Only fifteen years of age at the time, Tim's kindness toward older folks, his technical skills, and reasonable rates drew many clients his way. As BTPP went from a dream to a reality, Tim created the created the very first BTPP website, the BTPP Facebook group, and much more. All these years later, now living in Seattle and married to the lovely Kathryn, they have helped launch the Tails from Beyond the Paw Print book.

Another interesting intersection of life brought Eric Keller into the Tails book project. I first met Eric at a family gathering, as he is married to my cousin, author and communication skills trainer, Laurie Brown. A quiet and modest individual, Eric never spoke about himself or his work. As I began my fledging project, I sought out the advice of local author and physician Dr. Howard Schubiner and asked if he could recommend an animal loving person who might be interested in handling the graphic design work for Tails. Without any hesitation, Dr. Schubiner recommended his friend, Eric. As he began to describe him, my initial reaction was...Could it be? Yes, it was the very same Eric! I believe these connections are more than a coincidence.

When it came time to choose just the right person to create the pet portraits, Eric recommended Hannah Tegan Johnson, illustrator and animal lover. Her pet portraits beautifully capture the essence of each companion featured in the stories. As Hannah's career progresses, which it surely will, I can say, "I knew her when ..." Then there's Eric's virtual partner, Arlene, who does a brilliant job of making each page of this book appear inviting to the eye. Near the end of the project, Arlene and her husband, Steve (a professional editor) also provided editing talents, which I truly appreciate. Although we have never met, I have discovered a kindred spirit in Arlene and am so glad she joined our team. Her upbeat personality and ready laugh were a welcome balm. Eric and Howard further referred me to Jennifer Riemenschneider at Sheridan Books. Jennifer has been terrific and has always responded with kindness, clear direction, and patience through the many phone calls and emails from this fledging author and self-publisher. I am also grateful to my editor-in-chief, Cindi Cook. I first met Cindi when she attended a BTPP meeting in search of support over the death of her beloved dog, Lila. I am very grateful that we were brought together by BTPP. Her firsthand experience with the group was a gift and Cindi handled the 22 stories with both tender and professional care.

I owe a debt of gratitude to Jennifer Cote, retired chairwoman of the Department of Paralegal Studies at Madonna University. As a witness to my grief after the deaths of both parents, Jennifer encouraged me to reach out to her colleague, Dr. Kelly Rhoades, chairwoman of the department of Hospice and Palliative Studies at Madonna University. Aware of my past connection to the academic environment, as both a student and instructor, Jennifer thought I might be drawn to this particular program and find meaning in the coursework. I made the call and an appointment was set.

When I entered the office of Dr. Kelly Rhoades, I was certain I had taken a wrong turn in the maze of offices. Why? The woman who stood up to greet me wasn't dressed in black, neither did she look sad or grief-stricken. The woman standing before me was a stunning blonde, dressed in a brightly colored suit, with a kind and welcoming smile. More important, I sensed I was in the company of someone who appeared happy. In the midst of those initial moments, I wondered how someone enmeshed in the field of hospice and bereavement could appear so full of life and yes, stylish? In absence of the facts, I found myself engaged in stereotyping about the program and founder. My education in the Hospice and Palliative Studies program began with that first meeting as did my journey toward healing. I had found my mentor.

I remain indebted to Jennifer Cote for her ongoing encouragement to reach out to Dr. Rhoades. Without her interest, kindness and intervention, my story would have turned out differently. Entering this unique graduate program, with a concentration in Bereavement Studies changed my life.

This program changed my life in three specific ways: I confronted my losses, founded Beyond the Paw Print, and found myself one step closer toward becoming a hospital chaplain. All these years later, I am grateful that Dr. Rhoades generously agreed to write the Foreword to this book. A treasured mentor, her insights and suggestions throughout the writing of this book, were invaluable.

In my early research on pet loss, I was struck by the number of authors and scholars who have specialized in this subject (a selection of these titles can be found in the Bibliography section of this book). I am fortunate to have connected with Dr. Wallace Sife, author of The Loss of a Pet and founder of the online group, The Association for Pet Loss and Bereavement. Just prior to the publication of this book, I received the very sad news that Dr. Sife died on April 8, 2020, in Brooklyn, N.Y. We have lost our greatest advocate. From my first phone call to him back in 2008, Dr. Sife was warm, open, and supportive of my research on pet loss. I remember my excitement when he agreed to publish the first version of Pablo's story in his Winter 2009 online newsletter. I will remain forever grateful for his ongoing support of BTPP and, most recently, his enthusiastic review of this book.

Another wonderful outcome of being a part of this academic experience was the friendship that developed with classmate, Patty Merlo. During our final semester, we discovered that we shared identical plans for the summer: an internship in a clinical pastoral education program at a local hospital system. I was delighted to start my chaplain intern journey alongside Patty, and often felt that the intersection of our lives had to be more than a coincidence.

Throughout our chaplaincy training, and in the formation of BTPP, Patty has been a great friend and champion. As I began to outline my ideas for this book, Patty joined me from the start – a sounding board for all my ideas – with suggestions that have influenced its direction. As an enthusiastic reader and frequent editor of the stories, her belief in this book helped me persevere against all odds. Additionally, Patty wrote the Afterword which includes a beautiful meditation, accessible on the BTPP website. Beyond our work together, the icing on the cake was the opportunity to befriend her husband Tony Sr., and their four children, Laura, Lisa, Paul, and Tony.

Tony Merlo, Patty's son, willingly accepted the role of technical advisor formerly managed by Tim Carlson. He presently oversees BTPP's website, co-administrates the Facebook group, and provides support in a multitude of ways. His patience and kindness are traits most appreciated by both my husband, Bud and me.

Larry McLaughlin has freely provided legal expertise in a multitude of ways, and I couldn't be more grateful. Larry's time and expertise has made all the difference. His help in all aspects of the book writing and publishing process were invaluable. Larry and his dear wife, Patti have been close friends of ours for more than 25 years.

There are some very special medical care practitioners whose intervention made all the difference. Without them, I wouldn't have had the courage and determination to turn my dream into a reality. I first met Dr. Ken Peters in the autumn of 1996, when he was a Resident Fellow at a local hospital system. His expertise, positive outlook, effective listening skills, and kindness toward his now massive patient population make all the difference. When my symptoms reoccurred after nearly twenty pain-free years, his openminded approach revealed another possibility and root cause for my symptoms. Two years ago, Dr. Peters urged me to meet with Dr. Howard Schubiner (unlearnyourpain.com), which has been the greatest of gifts, and this book is the outcome.

Dr. Schubiner's caring approach and unique program provide troubled souls the opportunity to rediscover hope and healing. Who would have thought that such a program exists?

This book would have remained an unfulfilled dream, were it not for his Unlearn Your Pain program. I often pinch myself at this achievement, especially when my lack of confidence, anxiety, and fear often threatened to sabotage my efforts. The process hasn't been easy. The journey has been full of unforeseen challenges and unexpected twists and turns But the dream has been achieved. His program works!

Along the way, some of these practitioners became treasured friends: Luisa DiLorenzo, Amy Drean, Reid Kavieff (wife Cindy), Mike Pizzimenti, David Rosman (wife Marla), all have hearts of gold, the patience of Job, and are true advocates on behalf of their patients. Many thanks to Luisa De Lorenzo's team: Lynn Park Bennett, Deborah Geralin Hart, Amanda Sundus Jihad, Dr. Sue Lim, Danielle Mayne, Tina Marie Stefani.

Throughout different time periods and critical junctures in my life, the following individuals provided much needed insight and understanding. They helped make sense of some of life's most confounding questions. Moreover, they helped me confront, process, and understand the grief I sought to deny. Their genuine kindness, compassion and support, made the journey less frightening. Thank you Elana Goell, Toby Hazan, Debra Hollander, Lila Massoumi, and Sally Palaian.

After my high school counselor informed my parents that, in his estimation, I did not possess the necessary skills or aptitude to succeed in college, I enrolled at one of the local campuses of Oakland Community College (OCC). The teachers were excellent, and much to my amazement, I graduated with honors. My OCC guidance counselor, Dr. Roger Zapinski, encouraged me to reach for the stars and apply to universities out-of-state. I had always dreamed of attending school in Boston, but never believed it was a realistic goal. With the encouragement of Dr. Zapinksi, I applied and was accepted at Emerson College. I moved to Boston and began the second half of my undergraduate studies at this premier institution in the field of communication. With acceptance into this college, I hit the Golden Buzzer – that's for sure! As Emerson College founder, Charles Wesley Emerson (cousin of Ralph Waldo Emerson) said in 1880, "Expression Necessary to Evolution," and he wasn't kidding. It's true.

While a graduate student at Emerson, Dr. Mark McPhail became a close friend and mentor whose love of speech communication inspired me to pursue a career in academia. Mark was a brilliant professor and inspired his students to appreciate the educational experience awarded us. I am indebted to Dr. McPhail and other professors which include Ph.D.s, Toby Berkowitz, Kevin Greeley, Andy Rancer, and Allan Silvestri who encouraged me to apply for doctoral programs in speech communication. When I expressed a desire to return to Michigan to be near my parents, first on our list was Wayne State University. Fortunately, I was accepted into the university's Department of Communication. Thank you, Dr. Bernard Brock (in memoriam), Dr. Mark McPhail (who later joined the faculty), Dr. Larry Miller, and Dr. Matt Seeger, and many others who influenced my formation as a critical thinker, writer, and instructor.

While completing my doctorate at WSU, I met and began dating my future husband, Bud. During our courtship, Bud's job led to an overseas assignment in Europe. When we married a few months later, Pablo, Nellie, Isabella and I joined him to begin this new chapter in our lives.

Our new life as a married couple in London, England were equal parts excitement and adjustment. While I sought to find my footing, I regularly pinched myself that our new life together wasn't one big dream. As we acclimated to this new life, I had the opportunity to broaden my horizons by volunteering at a variety of organizations which permitted me to meet people from all different cultures and religious affiliations. I volunteered at the English-Speaking Union in the conversational English program where I had the privilege of interacting with individuals from a variety of foreign countries.

Seeking additional opportunities to get involved with our new community, I reached out to St. Wilfrid's Catholic Home for the Aged where Bud and I served as volunteers under the tutelage of our beloved friend, Sister Margaret McMullen. We found a home and family among the sisters and residents and are very grateful for the relationships formed.

I learned about Nightingale House, a Jewish home for the aged, through a newspaper article. It sounded like a wonderful place and after being interviewed, I became a volunteer in the social activities department. Through these voluntary experiences at the English-Speaking Union, St. Wilfrid's, and Nightingale House, I become a more compassionate and empathic listener. At the time, I did not anticipate that these skills would be called upon later in my life.

In addition to the relationships mentioned above, we encountered some wonderful individuals who welcomed this newlywedded couple in their lives: Don (who passed away on March 10, 2020) and his wife Noelene Hewitson, former proprietors of the Cork and Bottle and Hanover Square Wine bar; Ffiona, proprietor of Ffiona's restaurant in Kensington; Nino, Pietro and Paula, of Assaggi restaurant in Notting Hill.

Our reverence for the beautiful coastline of Southwest Cornwall led us to the village of St. Mawes, and The Tresanton Hotel. Over several visits, proprietor and hotelier, Olga Polizzi and her husband, author William Shawcross took the time to become better acquainted with us. We were struck by the genuine kindness of these larger than life individuals and are delighted to remain connected. Frequent visits to St. Mawes led to a friendship with resident painter and local historian Yvonne Fuller, who often accompanied us on our walks along the gorgeous coast and countryside.

I never anticipated the path that lay before me after

our repatriation to the United States. Neither did I imagine a return to the academic world as a student of hospice and palliative care, or that I would pursue training in the field of hospital chaplaincy. After graduation with my degree in Hospice and Palliative Studies, I was delighted when Reverend Dave Koch and Reverend Tony Marshall accepted me into their clinical pastoral education program at a regional hospital system. Their guidance, supervision, and encouragement helped shape my understanding of what it means to be a chaplain. Their supervisory sessions were legendary, and my classmates and I bonded over the cross examinations of our blind spots and biases.

After completing my chaplaincy internship in 2011, Dr. Beverly Beltramo took a chance and I landed my first job as a hospital staff chaplain. Through Bev, I found another mentor. Bev role-modeled the traits that inspired each of us to do our best. She was a wonderful leader, who recognized potential in each member of her staff, even if we were unable to visualize our own possibilities. Though we no longer work together, a friendship has flourished, and I continue to be the beneficiary of her wisdom. In addition, Bev's suggestions and edits for my introduction and the Afterword (by Patty Merlo) were invaluable. I am very grateful for her encouragement, time, and interest in the development of this book. Since Bev's departure, Kelly Heron has taken on the role of Chief Mission Officer, and I'm grateful for her encouragement, leadership, and genuine kindness.

I have much gratitude to my spiritual care colleagues – past and present. Working with them has brought continued learning and formation: Marianne Burnett, Kusalagnana Thero Derangala, Yvonne Foreman-Cannon, Mike Harning, Xchoi Hunt, Father Luke Iwuji, Patricia Johnson, Charles Kibiridge, Theresa Krell, Father Gary Morelli, Laurie O'Meara, Jacquie Patt, Susan Pawlos, Brian Shaffer, Barb Stevens, Vonna Strait, Linda Thompson, Heather Wilson. In memory of beloved classmate and colleague, Reverend Diane Smalley, who is greatly missed.

Dear Mom, Sylvia Burnstine Golden, there isn't a day where I don't mention her name, or my heart doesn't ache over her absence. Quite simply she was the very best mom and best friend. There was no better advisor, counselor, cheerleader, and teacher. She loved Bud and his son Ryan, and always reminded me of how fortunate I was to share my life with them. Her wisdom and insights were respected by all who knew her. I miss her deeply. I am grateful for the example she set on what mattered most — love. Her influence and legacy are infused in my every breath.

My love and appreciation for the great outdoors and the animal kingdom, came through my mom and dad. Whether taking time to join them in the cultivation of their flower and vegetable gardens, taking notice of the springtime buds on the apple trees, or the changing colors of the leaves in the Autumn season, I learned early on, to be mindful of the gracious gifts of our planet. I wasn't there to meet my dad's childhood dog, Beauty, but I was there for his last dog, Patches. I hope he shared a joyous reunion with both of them in the afterlife, in which he so strongly believed.

My dad, Lou Golden, struggled throughout his youth to help support his mother and three sisters. And, like many other young men of his era, sought to obtain the American dream. Though his early years were very difficult, his unwavering optimism, keen intellect, and sheer determination helped him achieve success on his own terms. As a young man, he aspired to be a sport's columnist for any of the Detroit newspaper outlets, or a pitcher for the Detroit Tigers. Instead, his magnetic personality enabled him to establish his own company. Dad always said, "I'm not a salesman, I'm a storyteller." His stories were legendary and always included lessons he had learned about life and its hidden meanings. A philanthropist in his later years, he supported a variety of organizations, but was happiest in Israel, at Haifa University, where he served on the Board of Governors and funded the Louis H. Golden cafeteria.

Dad often recalled those early days in his life when food was scarce, as were other creature comforts. He firmly believed that sustenance was necessary for optimal productivity. I couldn't agree more and am grateful to the following restaurants for feeding my imagination, body and spirit with their warm welcomes and delicious food:

- Bacco Ristorante and Bigalora Wood Fired Cucina: Proprietor Luciano Del Signore and his team, including Agata Lombardo Bogle, Elena Cacovean, Kelly Fink, Monica Iclodean, Kari Kennedy, Arthur Kudoshev, Andrew Lindhurst, Albert Ljucovic, Christine McKay, Kasha Matusinski
- Bella Piatti: Proprietors, Liz and Nino Cutraro and their team, including, Francesco Apollonia, Andrea Marquez DeLeon, Asraf and Afjal Hussan, Karl King, Kevin Mazziotta, James Schulz, Colin Solano, Bruce Vickery.
- Hong Hua: Proprietors, Shek Wei Seeto, Gary Yau, Danny Yu, and their team including, Peter Chan, Bo Szeto, Yiyao Wu, Fanny Yan.
- Jagged Fork: Proprietor Radu Trifon and his lovely wife Joanna.
- Lelli's: Proprietor Mark Zarkin, his lovely sweetheart, Fran, multi-talented son Ari, and their team including Faouzi, Lorenzo, Sanford, and Scott.
- Tam-O-Shanter: Proprietor Sheldon Yellen and his lovely mom Lenore Yellen. Many thanks to the Tam team which includes Ivan Avila, Monico Avila, Laurie Best, Michael Cohen, Marc Faranso, Lora Grimaldi, Carol Henson, Sheldon Jabero, Scott Jacobs, Scott Morrison, Lois Paquin-Hoffiz, Casey Philo, Marla Spaulding, Danielle Thomas, Anna Tobia, Bashar Tobia, Chris Wofford, Andy Yono, Antoinette Zangara.

With love and gratitude for my stepson Ryan, wife Dulcie, her parents Peggy and Andre Getty, Ryan's mom Donna

Moore, and two grandchildren, Coen and Zoey, along with their beloved cats, Stella, Sid and Lia.

Cary Moore: Son, brother, grandson, friend, and coach. His life, though way too short, mattered to many, both young and old. Cary will always be loved and remembered. His memory is honored through an annual college scholarship and the North Farmington High School press box, both of which are in his name. His legacy lives on through his brother Ryan and family. Cary's "granny" Rosemary loved and adored her grandsons and felt privileged when their dad asked her to help care for the boys. Rosemary often told me those were the best days of her life.

With gratitude to my immediate and extended families: My siblings, the Goldens: Stephen, Katherine, Andrew and his former wife Becky and their children Adam, Sydney and Sabra & her husband Dave and children Liam and Ella. Aunt Vera (in memoriam) and Uncle Izzy (in memoriam) Weinberg and their children, cousins Gary and Violetta, Larry and Louise, Gayle Harte, husband Elliott Greenburg and Gayle's daughters, Lauren and Joanna Steinhardt. Cousins Judy and Mort Levin, and their children Alissa and Jared & his wife Lora; Aunt Dorris and Uncle Maurice Chandler and their children, cousins Debby and Jonah, Evelyn (and Steve, in memoriam), Jerry and Paige, Paul and Chika; Aunt Lucille (in memoriam) and Uncle Lou Wonboy (in memoriam) and their children, cousins Cathy, Rick, and Ron and his wife Sarah.

During the latter part of my mom's life, she became especially close with her cousin, Florence Schuman. After mom's death, Florence informed me that "we were family," and she would always have a place for us at her table for every religious holiday. Florence kept her word till the day she died. Through Florence and her sister Helen, I became acquainted with a new generation of relatives. Many thanks to Susie Klau, Robin and Gary Wine, along with their daughters, Carly and Jaimee (aka Rivkah) and her husband, Oren. Laurie and husband Eric, Manny and wife Loretta, Robert and wife Lauri along with their children, Avery, Erica and Samantha.

Many thanks to the following friends and organizations, who have provided support in more ways than they will ever know:

Rochelle Adler, Jillian Berger (owner), Angie Kaufman, Regina Pipia, each gracious and kind friends of Ruby's Balm.

Lisette Benjamin and sons Dean, Jeremy, and Alon. Sue and Aaron Levine, Kit Chambers and Jeff Finn. Elizabeth Cobb. The Jewish Chaplaincy Network, Rabbi Benny and Bluma Greenwald of the Friendship Circle, Adat Shalom Synagogue, Temple Kol Ami, Woodward Avenue Shul.

Raimonda Gjekaj Pepaj and husband Benny, Robert and wife Dorrie Gjekai, Ella Gjekai, Bena Gjekai, Rachel Kopczynski, Zev and Vera Gjekai.

Fiaz and Juliana Al Maki, Ann Hwier, Bonita Seman.

Rick and Jorja Hanna, Sharad and Liz Jain, Mark and Jody Kosman.

Brenda and Mark Altus, Barbara Kaplan, Leslie Swartz, Lonny and Gail Zimmerman, BJ and Gary Berkowitz, Monica Del Signore, Jeff Fill, Alecia Gerosa, Beverly Ross and Robert Halperin, George Jackson, Dolores Levey and Ken Hart, Joanna and Radu Trifon, Kathryn and Robert Jacobs.

Becky and Will Haines, Evan and Renata McLaughlin, Kyle and Elizabeth McLaughlin, Larry McLaughlin Senior.

Joe Del Giudice, Gary Wachler, and David Wachler, each of whom helped make the publication of this book possible.

Dr. Ray Skowronksi and team Amber, Kim, Lori, Susan.

Dr. Jeffrey Fantich and team Ashley, Chris, Cindy, Jennifer.

Dr. Scott Owens and team Debby, Ellen, Jackie, Oana Paula, Sue.

Joanna Dyakowska, we are grateful for your presence in our lives. In memory of Joanna's beloved sister, Renata Dyakowska Formisano, and niece, Emili Formisano of Reggio Emilia, Italy.

In memory of dear friend, Karen Rappaport.

In memory of our very best friend, Jerry Poe. Shortly after meeting the man who would become my husband, I was introduced to his friend of fifty years and understood that he was part of the package. What a gift! Jerry infused our life with laughter and joy. His humor was the best, his storytelling legendary, his ability to bring joy to the life of my husband Bud was the greatest gift of all. I am forever grateful to my former cat-loving neighbor Gary Zebowski and dear friend Manuel Chavez, whose friendship set the stage for Bud and I to meet.

The very best for last … My husband, Carl (Bud) Moore. From the day we met, I knew he was the one for me. It may not be politically correct to say this, but he was and remains, my knight in shining armor. Though he didn't arrive on a horse, he drove a Ford Mustang! He is my everything and I love him with all my heart. He has never wavered in his support of any of my endeavors or dreams. I am grateful for his patience and participation in every stage of the compiling, editing, and writing of this book. He is my loving partner and very best friend. To our adored animal companions, Cornwall and Chelsea, we are so happy that we rescued each other! They bring so much joy into our lives… we love them so!

I will conclude where my life and Pablo's story began, with a mention of Lake Angelus, where I spent the first eleven years of my life. I came to appreciate the beauty and bounty of Mother Nature from this magical place. I am further grateful to have been introduced to the joys of animal companionship through the barnyard cats and horses that belonged to our next-door neighbor. These early childhood experiences among the animals and the lake have led me to where I am today, and for that I am and always will be eternally grateful.

Selected Resources on Pet Loss and Healing

Anderson Allen, Moira (2009). *Coping with Sorrow on the Loss of Your Pet* (Third Edition). Kearney: Morris Publishing.

Carmack, Betty (2002). *Grieving the Death of a Pet.* Minneapolis: Augsburg Fortress.

Carrison, Dan (2010). *Bill at Rainbow Bridge: Written for Owners of Departed Pets.* Santa Clarita: Modern Family Classics Publishing.

Dolan-Del, Ken & Nancy Saxton-Lopez (2013). *The Pet Loss Companion.* North Charleston: CreateSpace.

Ellis, Coleen (2011). *Pet Parents: A Journey Through Unconditional Love and Grief.* Bloomington: IUniverse, Inc.

Findlay, Linda B. & Roberts, David J. (2009). *Mourning Discoveries: A Guide to help Families Navigate Through Grief Towards Healing after the Loss of a Pet.* Whitesboro: Mourning Discoveries.

Francisco, Wendy (2010). *God and Dog.* New York: Center Street.

Greene, Lorri. A. & Landis, Jacquelyn (2002). *Saying Goodbye to the Pet You Love: A Complete Guide to Help You Heal*. Oakland: New Harbinger Publications.

Hanson, Warren (2008). *Paw Prints in the Stars: A Farewell and Journal for a Beloved Pet*. Minneapolis: Tristan.

Harrison, Susan (2015). *Going on a Journey*. Kalamazoo: Palamazoo.

Heegaard, Marge Eaton (2001). *Saying Goodbye to Your Pet: Children Can Learn to Cope with Pet Loss*. Minneapolis: Fairview Press.

Kaplan, Laurie (2010). *So Easy to Love So Hard to Lose: A Bridge to Healing Before and After the Loss of a Pet*. Briarcliff Manor: JanGen Press.

Katz, Jon (2012). *Going Home: Finding Peace When Pets Die*. New York: Random House.

Korpi, Sid (2009). *Good Grief: Finding Peace After Pet Loss*. Minneapolis: Healy House Books.

Kowalski, Gary (2012). *Goodbye, Friend: Healing Wisdom for Anyone Who has Ever Lost a Pet*. Novato: New World Library.

Lewis, Clive Staples (1961, 1989). *A Grief Observed*. Harper: San Francisco.

Montgomery, Mary & Montgomery, Herb (1999). *Goodbye My Friend: Grieving the Loss of a Pet*. Minneapolis: Montgomery Press.

Montgomery, Sy (2018). *How to be a Good Creature: A Memoir in Thirteen Animals*. Boston: Houghton Mifflin Harcourt.

Neruda, Pablo (1924, 1976). *Twenty Love Poems and a Song of Despair*. New York: Penguin.

Oliver, Mary (2013). *Dog Songs*. New York: Penguin.

O'Neill, Eugene (1940, re-issued 2014). *The Last Will and Testament of an Extremely Distinguished Dog*. Carlisle: Applewood.

Pomerance, Diane (2006). *Finding Peace after the Loss of a Loved Animal Companion*. Flower Mound: Polaire.

Reynolds, Rita M. (2000). *Blessing the Bridge: What Animals Teach Us About Death, Dying and Beyond*. Troutdale, Oregon: New Sage Press.

Robinett, Kristy (2018). *Tails from the Afterlife: Stories of Signs, Messages & Inspiration from your Animal Companions*. Woodbury: Llewellyn.

Schubiner, Howard (2016). *Unlearn Your Pain: A 28-Day Process to Reprogram your Brain* (Third edition). Pleasant Ridge: Mind Body.

Schwiebert, Pat and DeKlyen, Chuck (2010). *Tear Soup: A Recipe for Healing After Loss*. Portland: Grief Watch.

Shonk, B.J. (2017). *Missing Pieces Broken Heart: A Recovery Guide for the Grief and Sorrow of Pet Loss*. Middleton, DE: BJ Randolph.

Sife, Wallace (2014). *The Loss of a Pet: A Guide to Coping with the Grieving Process When a Pet Dies* (Fourth edition). New York: Howell Book House.

Stang, Heather (2018). *Mindfulness and Grief: Guided Meditations to Calm Your Mind and Restore Your Spirit*. London: CICO.

Traisman, Enid Samuel (1996). *My Personal Pet Remembrance Journal*. Portland: Dove Lewis.

Weller, Francis (2015). *The Wild Edge of Sorrow: Rituals of Renewal and the Sacred Work of Grief*. Berkeley: North Atlantic Books.

Williams, Margery (1922, 1995). *The Velveteen Rabbit*. Heinemann: London.

Wintz, Jack (2011). *Will I See My Pet in Heaven?* Brewster: Paraclete.

Wolfelt, Alan (2004). *When Your Pet Dies: A Guide to Mourning, Remembering and Healing*. Fort Collins: Companion Press.

PET LOSS BOOKS FOR CHILDREN

Gut, Corey (2014). *Being Brave for Bailey*. Signature Book Printing, www.sbpbooks.com.

Gut, Corey (2017). *Staying Strong for Smokey.* Signature Book Printing, www.sbpbooks.com.

Harrison, Susan (2015). *Going on a Journey*. Kalamazoo: Palamazoo.

Heegaard, Marge Eaton (2001). *Saying Goodbye to Your Pet.* Fairview: Minneapolis.

Hemery, Kathleen (2000). *Not Just a Fish*. Omaha: Centering Corporation.

Karst, Patrice (2000). *The Invisible String*. DeVorss: Camarillo.

Krantz, Heather (2018). *Bubble Trouble: Using Mindfulness to Help Kids with Grief*. Bend, Oregon: Herow Press.

Liss-Levinson, Nechama and Molly Phinney Baskette (2007). *Remembering My Pet: A Kid's Own Spiritual Workbook for When a Pet Dies*. Woodstock: Skylight Paths.

Rhoades, Kelly (2009). *Quilly's Sideways Grief.* Marco Publishing (marcoproducts.com). New Bern: Marco.

Rylant, Cynthia *(1995)*. *Dog Heaven*. New York: Blue Sky Press.

Rylant, Cynthia (1997). *Cat Heaven*. New York: Blue Sky Press.

Thomas, Pat (2012). *I Miss My Pet: A First Look at When a Pet Dies*. London: Barron's Educational Series.

Tousley, Marty (1996). *Children and Pet Loss: A Guide for Helping*. Phoenix: Our Pals Publishing.

Van-Si, Laurie (2014). *Saying Goodbye to my Awesome Pet: An Activity Book for the Grieving Child*. Essential Insights.

Viorst, Judith (1971). *The Tenth Good Thing About Barney*. New York: Aladdin.

SELECTED WEBSITES ON PET LOSS

Association of Pet Loss and Bereavement   www.aplb.org

Beyond the Paw Print www.beyondthepawprint.com

Colorado State University   www.argusinstitute.colostate.edu

Crossroads Veterinary Hospice   crossroadsvethospice.com

Grief Healing   www.griefhealing.com/petlinks.htm

In Memory of Pets   www.in-memory-of-pets.com

Michigan State University   www.cvm.msu.edu/petloss/index.htm

Nikki Hospice Foundation for Pets   www.pethospice.org

Pet Grief Support and Candle Ceremony   www.petloss.com

Pet Loss Support Page   www.pet-loss.com

Rainbow Bridge Poem and More www.RainbowBridge.com

University of California-Davis   www.vetmed.ucdavis.edu/petloss/

Washington State University   www.vetmed.wsu.edu/PLHL/home/

Tails Team

Tim and Kathryn Carlson

THE CARLSON FAMILY AND THEIR DOG NGUYA, met Micky, Bud and their cats Pablo, Isabella and Nellie, when they moved into the house across the street in the summer of 2007. Mary Lynn delivered flyers to the mailboxes of near neighbors advertising her son's business venture, Carlson's Computing Services, which Tim founded at the age of fifteen. Micky was his first client! A close friendship developed between the Carlson's and the Moore's, which came to include pet sitting — when either family traveled out of town.

MR. DARCY

An integral part of BTPP from its inception, Tim played a key role in developing the initial BTPP website, had the vision to extend the group beyond physical meetings to include a social media presence, and co-created a variety of power point presentations which Micky used to lecture vet clinics on supporting pet loss clients. After high school, Tim attended Seattle Pacific University, where he met his future wife, Kathryn Wange. After completing his MSc. in Finance at Duisenberg School of Finance in Amsterdam, Tim made a permanent move to Seattle, all the while staying in touch with Micky and Bud.

For this project, Kathryn and Tim worked with Micky on the technical set up to list the book for sale, developing the product page and optimizing for discoverability and search rankings. As a team, Tim is a natural with computers and analytics, and Kathryn specializes in marketing and program management.

Kathryn and Tim Carlson live in Seattle, WA, and love traveling, cooking, and gardening. They both work at Amazon, and their miniature goldendoodle, Mr. Darcy, accompanies them to the office every day. After a long day of naps, hugs, and treats at work, Mr. Darcy enjoys chasing tennis balls and watching movies in bed.

Cindi Cook, Editor

CINDI COOK IS A WRITER AND EDITOR whose work has appeared in *The New York Times, Women's Wear Daily, Tatler, Allure, Conde Nast Traveler, teNeues, The New York Post, Daily Candy, NYLON, Manhattan File, Hamptons, and Hamptons Country.* Ms. Cook runs the editorial production company CCC which takes on creative projects of all kinds. She has launched three magazines and headed three start-ups of both local and national publications. Ms. Cook has two children's books in the works, *Josephine and the Yellow Umbrella* about a little girl in Paris, and *Pink Bone*, the story of Lila, her beloved Rhodesian Ridgeback/Shepherd mix, who came into her life four years ago and unfortunately exited it last year. Ms. Cook has also shared a household with cats Muffin, Sebastian, Honey, Minnie, and Rubin, all of whom have touched her heart. Ms. Cook resides in Paris and Detroit and is looking forward to welcoming a new canine companion soon.

LILA

Eric Keller, Graphic Designer

CATS AND DOGS. They have been an enormous part of my world. Sometimes I even frame my life in terms of the cats and dogs I have known: "Oh yeah, was that back when Otis was still a puppy?" or "That was around the time when Bella found us."

I've had the pleasure of living with Melba, Otis, Minou, Beau, Monte, Skye, Mookie (and her three puppies), Mushka, Miko, Levi, and my current crew: my cats Lola, Otto and Bella, and my dogs Kaya and Jake.

KAYA

With the joy they bring to us, eventually, they also bring heartache. Inspired by my own history of love and loss, I feel honored to work with Micky, Hannah, and Cindi to help create *Tails from Beyond the Paw Print: Stories of Love, Loss and Lessons Learned from our Adored Animal Companions*. I'm grateful to have the opportunity to express my love for dogs and cats in a meaningful way: by using my skills as a graphic designer and art director. In addition to books, I also design logos, websites, and marketing material and have been involved in a number of start-ups. Mostly, I work with non-profits involved in healthcare, education, and the arts. Recently, I designed branding for a non-profit that uses advances in genomics to breed vapor dogs – the dogs you see at airports, stadiums, and arenas doing pretty serious detection work. You can see more of my work at erickellerdesign.com.

JAKE

I also have a website, thedogsihaveknown.com, that features my drawings and very short stories about dogs, and sometimes, in a way, about people too.

Speaking of dogs, when I'm not working, my favorite thing to do is to team up with my dog Jake who is a therapy dog. Jake and I visit hospitals and a Detroit elementary school, where we help kids learn to read. It's a good way for me and Jake to help people—and keeps Jake pretty busy too.

Hannah Tegan, Illustrator

As an artist and illustrator, I have had the opportunity to work on a variety of projects, from creating logos for new businesses to painting family portraits. Four years ago, after the death of a close friend's dog, I felt compelled to create a portrait of his pet that might express my condolences as well as offer a lasting tribute. My friend and his family were very grateful to receive this portrait, and their reaction encouraged me to try my hand at pet portraits. I discovered that I love doing them! Interest in my work grew, and I am blessed to have pet portrait clients from all over the world. The creative process begins when I draw a sketch of a pet based on the pictures sent to me from the owners. After the sketching process, most of my pieces are mixed media works of watercolor, ink, and colored pencil. Once my signature circle background is painted in and my initials carefully placed, it is sent off.

EMMA

When the opportunity arose to create the illustrations for this project, I was delighted! Through the stories and photographs I received, I felt as though I knew each companion intimately; which helped me create portraits that highlight each animal's personality and physical likeness. Throughout this project, I found myself reflecting on the companions I have loved and lost. I often think of my two rescue pups, Maddie, the Wheaton terrier, and Rocky, the Cairn terrier, as well as our sweet tuxedoed feline JD. These pets were by my side through my own loss and heartache, on the best and worst days. Currently, we are enjoying a Blue Heeler rescue dog named Emma, who is living her glory days as a part of the Johnson Family. She is a perfect match for our two sons, Atticus and Gideon. I am so happy to see the loving bond that has developed between the three of them, especially the wrestling matches!

In addition to pet portraits, I create custom pieces of art in many forms. My work can be seen on my website, www.hannahtegan.com, and my Instagram page, @htegan, is a safe and inspiring space for mothers who are artists.

Arlene Cohn, Production Design

I WAS NEVER A CAT PERSON. Both my husband and I grew up with dogs. I always believed that when I got a pet for my own family, it would be a dog. But life plays tricks on you.

I started my career as an IT guru. When I was burned out by corporate America, I joined my husband in his one-person speaking/training business. Our roles were very clear. He got up on stage. I did everything else — except sales. We both hated sales. So, it was no surprise when he accepted a full-time position with a consulting company.

Now I'm a Virtual Assistant, helping people do almost anything they need to run their business (except sales). Working in PJs from my Atlanta home office, I do everything from Microsoft Office tasks to a little graphic design to book layout. That's how I started to work with Eric. He designs the overall look of the book, and I design how it's laid out for print. Although we've never met in person, we've worked on several book projects together. As a matter of fact, Micky and I haven't met in person either, but I feel we have a connection through our mutual love of animals.

ARLO

I have two wonderful daughters. Unfortunately, they both have A.D.D. (and so does my husband). There was no way I could take care of another living creature while they were younger.

Then they both moved out and my husband began traveling a lot for work and I was alone much of the time. The girls, who both had cats, convinced me to adopt a neighborhood stray cat that had always been hanging around our house since he was a kitten. He was very sweet and let anybody pet him. They had even named him a few years back — "Precious" (they thought he was a she).

Since he lived his whole life outdoors, we installed a cat door so he could come and go whenever he wanted. He always came in at night. If he wasn't in the house by the time we went to bed, all we had to do was open the front door and call him. He always came immediately. He spent the night in our bed at my feet.

Precious kept me company when I was home alone and loved to crawl into my lap to cuddle — so long as I put a pillow on my lap first. He'd stand and wait until I got the pillow, then he'd climb on.

I never believed I could love a cat so much!

There had been some talk of cayotes being sighted in the neighborhood. A few cats were attacked. And when Precious didn't come in one night when we called him, and still wasn't there in the morning, we knew. We searched for him. But we knew.

I was devastated!

My husband and I decided no more pets. The eventual loss was too overwhelming. That was almost two years ago ...

Then, a few months ago, while looking at my neighborhood online bulletin board, I saw a post about a little kitty in need of a home. This kind Samaritan explained that the little sweetheart was hanging around her property, looking tired and injured. The last straw was when she saw that he was walking on only three legs. She took him to the vet and paid for him to be boarded for three days to allow his leg to heal. With two cats of her own, she was not able to give him a home and started to look for someone to adopt him.

As I read her post, there were tears streaming down my face. He looked just like Precious! And he wasn't really an outdoor cat, so I couldn't lose him the same way I lost Precious. I called my husband in to read the post. He just sighed and looked at me and said, "If it will make you happy."

I brought Arlo home from the vet that afternoon.

Arlo (or Arlo "Cathrie" as my son-in-law calls him as a pun) is the light of our lives. He's so friendly and playful and just loves when we pet him.

If Arlo hadn't come into my life when he did, I'm not sure I could have worked on this book. With such a big hole in my heart, it would have been excruciatingly painful.

I didn't even realize just how large a hole there actually was in my heart until Arlo filled it!

Patty Merlo, M.P.M. Spiritual Director

EVER SINCE CHILDHOOD, my family members and our pets have been important friends and pillars of support for me. Queenie, our first dog, and Pepe, the pure-bred poodle that arrived next, became siblings who comforted me after my Mom's death when I was only eleven years old. Their unconditional love and companionship were invaluable to me while my Dad was grieving his own loss and learning to navigate as a single parent.

DARREN

Many years later, as a wife and mother of four children, our home was filled with guinea pigs, hamsters, turtles, fish, and a cat. My husband and I waited until our second child went to college before getting our first puppy, Darren, an adorable Pomeranian who quickly ruled as the new king of our family. He was so pampered (and adored) that even some neighbors included him in their family photos!

My life's journey led me into several helping professions — teacher, spiritual director, retreat facilitator, chaplain, and caregiver. I currently facilitate retreats on prayer and forgiveness and also work as a spiritual director helping people discern God's presence in their daily lives.

For the past year, I have been writing a book on Intercessory Prayer, and am very grateful for the comments and suggestions provided by those who have reviewed my early drafts.

For the past ten years, it has been a great honor and blessing to be a part of Micky's outreach to persons who both grieve the passing and also celebrate the love they received from their animal companions. When Micky first shared her idea for this book, I urged her to pursue this dream and have been delighted to serve as a proof reader and sounding board. It has been a joy to be a part of this project from its inception through completion. I welcome your comments through my website www.pattymerlo.com.

Tony Merlo, Technology Editor

TONY MERLO HAS WORKED in the tech industry for almost twenty years and is passionate about finding ways to use technology to create new experiences. Tony also enjoys traveling throughout the country teaching business management courses for the Professional Development Center of Lawrence Tech. Tony's love of teaching coupled with his practical experience and genuine interest in helping students believe in themselves makes him an instructor in demand.

ROXY

Tony is also a guitar player and songwriter who has collaborated with a variety of musicians throughout his career. Tony enjoys playing his guitar and singing to his biggest fan: his Pomeranian furry baby named Roxy. He is currently working with augmented reality www.roadmaptoar.com to create holograms of Roxy's happy and loving spirit. As a provider of tech support along with endless encouragement, the work that Tony did on this book is a tribute to Roxy and his first dog Darren (a.k.a. Fussy), may he rest in peace.

About Dr. Micky Golden Moore

DR. MICKY GOLDEN MOORE founded Beyond the Paw Print in 2009 after the deaths of her best feline friends, Pablo, Isabella, and Nellie. She found that pet loss grief was often misunderstood and marginalized, and sought to alter that perception. She created this group to provide support for those grieving the death of their beloved animal companions. Her extensive academic training and teaching background, a second career as a hospital chaplain, and her personal experience, make Dr. Golden Moore an ideal facilitator for a pet loss support group. Her caring and listening presence invite attendees to share their stories of love, loss, and lessons learned.

Tails from Beyond the Paw Print was published to commemorate the group's ten year anniversary of serving the greater Detroit pet loss community.

Dr. Golden Moore has a B.S. degree in Interpersonal Communication from Emerson College, (Boston, MA), two master's degrees — an M.A. in Organizational Communication from Emerson College and an M.S. in Hospice and Palliative Studies from Madonna University (Livonia, MI), and a Ph.D. in Speech Communication, Rhetoric & Public Address from Wayne State University (Detroit, MI).

Dr. Golden Moore currently works as a staff chaplain at a regional hospital in South Eastern Michigan — a career she chose after being on the receiving end of these services just before her dad's passing. Prior to becoming a chaplain, Dr. Golden Moore spent nearly thirty years as a university instructor.

Inspired by her parents, volunteer work is her passion. She hosts an annual Holiday Donation Drive every December called the "Beyond the Paw Print Gathering to Give" event. Past and present Beyond the Paw Print attendees come together to provide donations to a specially selected rescue organization in memory of their beloved animal companions. She received the Karmanos Cancer Institute Crystal Award Volunteer of the Year for establishing the Volunteer Speakers Bureau training program in Public Speaking. While living in London, England, Dr. Golden Moore volunteered at St. Wilfrid's Home for the Aged, Nightingale House and the English-Speaking Union.

Dr. Golden Moore lives near Detroit with her husband Bud and their rescue cats, Cornwall and Chelsea. Visit her online at beyondthepawprint.com, on the Beyond the Paw Print Pet Loss Support Group page on Facebook, and on Instagram at beyondthepawprint.